Echoes of the Dominator
The Tales and the Men Who Flew the B-32

ECHOES OF THE DOMINATOR

THE TALES AND THE MEN WHO FLEW THE B-32

Benjamin A. Sinko

Up North Press

Minneapolis, MN

Echoes of the Dominator
The Tales and the Men Who Flew the B-32

Editor: Stephanie Neubeck
Cover Design: Lila Lam
Book Layout: Benjamin Sinko
Cover Photo: Authors Collection

Up North Press
P.O. Box 49351
Blaine, MN 55449-0351
www.b32dominator.com
b32dominator@yahoo.com

ISBN - 978-0-6151-5898-3

I am always interested in updating to include as many personal accounts or photographs as possible, in my goal to present the story of the B-32 through the eyes of the men who were there. If there is information that you are interested in sharing for future revisions please contact me at the address or email address above.

Printed in the United States

For: My Dad, thank you for supporting me.

To: My Grandfathers and all
World War II Veterans. Thank you.

Contents

ACKNOWLEDGEMENTS   8
PREFACE   9

I - THE STARTING POINT
    CHAPTER 1 – MODEL NUMBER 33   13
    CHAPTER 2 – PRODUCTION   19
    CHAPTER 3 – DOMINATOR   33

II - PREPARING FOR WAR
    CHAPTER 4 – TESTING   39
    CHAPTER 5 – TRAINING   49

III - THE B-32 GOES TO WAR
    CHAPTER 6 - THE COOK PROJECT   63
    CHAPTER 7 - THE COOK REPORT   95
    CHAPTER 8 - 386th BS VERY HEAVY   105
    CHAPTER 9 - WARS END   133

APPENDIX I   143
APPENDIX II   144
APPENDIX III   145
BIBLIOGRAPHY   151

ACKNOWLEDGEMENTS

Without the support from the people below this dream could have never become a reality, Thank You!

Col. F.L. Svore (Ret), Wayne G. Grooms, Ken Eidnes, Roger Arendsee, Robert Kirk, Jack Munsell, Nita Fredrickson, Steven Albert, Justin Kossor and the Justin Museum of Military History, Minnesota Air & Space Museum. Also the research staffs at the San Diego Air and Space Museum, National Museum of the USAF and the United States Air Force Historical Research Center at Maxwell AFB. Also I would like to thank my family and friends for their continued support throughout this effort.

PREFACE

Information on the B-32 Dominator is almost as obscure as the airplane itself. In fact; prior to the summer of 2003, I had never even heard of the bomber, until reading a reference to it and curiosity set in immediately. I began searching everywhere for information exhausting what few resources were available. By the following summer I met the only unit commander of a B-32 combat squadron, a few veterans and their families who had never shared their stories before and compiled binders of information, but the question soon arose, what to do with all of my new found knowledge?

There was a compelling need within me to share these never before heard first hand accounts of the events that involved the men who flew with the Dominator in combat and in training. Using the official histories of the units who flew the B-32, flight manuals and personal narratives of the crew members the most complete account of the B-32's service life is presented in the pages that follow.

What is missing is an in depth study of technical information. If you are looking for more than this book offers, there is a great book by Stephan Harding and James Long entitled, *Dominator: The Consolidated B-32 Bomber*, published by Pictorial Histories of Missoula, Montana. This book offers an extensive amount of technical information on the B-32.

My goal with this book was to piece together the incomplete story of the B-32's brief combat career and to shed a new light on the overall history of the Dominator using a mostly untapped resource, the men whose lives were forever impacted by their association with the bomber. Vast holes in the history of the B-32 have been filled through the accounts of the men who were there; men such as the only combat commander, pilots involved in training programs and others with brief encounters with the bomber. A new interpretation of its short lived career is presented in the following pages.

THE STARTING POINT

CHAPTER 1

MODEL NUMBER 33

The saga of the Consolidated B-32 Dominator, and more importantly the men associated with the aircraft, is an often over looked portion of World War II history. The United States Army Air Force (USAAF) even kept the Dominator a secret until after the war and the bombers operation career had ended. This is surprising because the Dominator was involved with some of the most significant events during the last days of the war. The personal experiences fade with each passing day, and with the lack of a surviving example the history of the B-32 can only echo through time in the form of oral and written histories of the men who were there.

The history of the B-32 began on 10 November 1939, when the United States Army Air Corps (USAAC) issued specifications for a replacement for the Boeing B-17 Flying Fortress and the Consolidated B-24 Liberator bombers. The new bomber was required to have the ability to carry a 20,000 pound bomb load for a range of 5,333 miles at a maximum speed of 400 miles per hour. The final specification required the manufacturers to design an entirely new aircraft. Many people have referred to the B-32 as the "Giant Liberator" but the only similarity to the B-24 was the twin tail configuration.

The second XB-32 *41-142* on an early test flight (USAF)

41-142 sitting on the ramp at Muroc AAF between test flights, the extra fin on the aft fuselage was used to for stability tests. (USAF)

Consolidated Aircraft Corporation gave the bomber the product identification number model 33 and began design of the new aircraft on 5 November 1940. The final plans were submitted to the USAAC on 24 August 1940 and assigned the designation of bomber 32(B-32). On 6 September 1940 a contract was issued for two prototypes designated as XB-32's, a wind tunnel model and a technical data model. Two months later the order was increased to include a third XB-32.

The XB-32 was eighty three feet long and had a wingspan of 135 feet. It featured a twin tail design similar to the B-24 and press-urized crew compartments. It had a range of 4,450 miles and an average airspeed of 250 mph. For defensive armament there were two remotely operated retractable turrets. Each was armed with four .50 cal machine guns positioned in the midsection directly behind the bomb bay. The turret was operated by a fire control officer who used a periscope computing site to aim the turrets. To cover the rear of the bomber there was one .20 mm cannon and two .50 caliber machine guns in the rear portion of each the outboard engine nacelles. To cover the front there were two .50 caliber machine guns, one in each wing.

Rear view of *41-142*, the glass enclosure housed the tail gunner (USAF)

The engines were the same Pratt and Whitney R-3350's that were on the B-29 and turned a three bladed Hamilton Standard propeller.

The first XB-32 serial number *41-141* rolled off of Consolidated's San Diego production line on 3 September 1942. Six days later, on 9 September, *141* made its maiden flight, two weeks prior to the first flight of the B-29. When the test flights ended 9 May 1943, thirty flights had been made. On 10 May the test crew began to make its regular take off run down the runway. Just as the bomber lifted into the air and cleared the end of the airstrip it suddenly lost altitude and crashed just past the end of the runway killing a Consolidated test pilot and injuring six others onboard. The aircraft was a total loss.

Unfortunately with crash of *141*, which caused the loss of critical flying time and technical information, development was pushed back until the second XB-32 was completed allowing the test program to resume. Consolidated used *142* for the brunt of the testing to make up for the loss of the first XB-32. In the fall of 1943 it was transferred to Muroc AAF for load testing and evaluation of the specifications

The third XB-32 was fitted with a tail that resembling the one used on production B-32's. It was also fitted with a mock turret forward of the tail. (Consolidated)

Consolidated submitted to the renamed USAAF. While at Muroc AAF the weight of the XB-32, 101,622 pounds. became problematic. The test crews experienced issues achieving designated speeds and the required range. It was at this time the USAAF began to make decisions about the future design of the XB-32.

The final XB-32 serial number *41-013886* was completed on 9 November 1943 and was delivered to the United States Army Air Force at Wright Field for further testing. The third test model was completed identically to the previous two. Eventually, the third XB-32 was modified with a single tail to increase stabilization. Throughout testing new design modifications were evaluated on this aircraft prior to being implemented during production.

CHAPTER 2

PRODUCTION

The final production version of the B-32 was dramatically different than the XB-32. Officially, production was scheduled to begin during the summer of 1943. The USAAF had earmarked the B-32 for use in Europe, to replace B-17 and B-24 units starting in the Mediterranean and then those stationed in England by wars' end. Army Air Force officials felt that the Dominator was better suited for Europe because of its smaller size and the required length of runway for take off and landing was shorter than that of the B-29. Production proved to be an ongoing set of challenges and changes. A host of setbacks in production led to many struggles with the bomber being accepted by the USAAF which also meant that the B-32 would arrive too late to be deployed in Europe and would just start reaching the Pacific theater by VJ Day.

On 4 March 1943 the first contract was issued by the USAAF for 300 B-32's. Consolidated chose their Fort Worth production facility to build the Dominator, even though all three XB-32's had been built at the San Diego facility. Included in the initial order was a stipulation that forty aircraft were to be produced as TB-32's for use in training

B-32's nearing completion on the production line. The Consolidated plant at Fort Worth was a mile long. (Consolidated)

TB-32's very near completion, similar to the combat model except for the deletion of all defensive armament. (USAF)

new crews. The TB-32 was essentially a B-32 without defensive armament and the addition of ballast weight in the rear of the aircraft to compensate for the missing weight. The TB-32's were to take priority; as soon as the required test models were completed. The training versions were built prior to the completion of combat equipped production models.

Then on 26 August 1943, as production was set to begin, the USAAF issued an extensive list of design modifications to be implemented prior to production. Due to the changes pressed on Consolidated late in the development stage the first B-32 was now not scheduled to be completed until April 1944, nine months later than had been originally scheduled.

The ordered design modifications resulted in the B-32 being renumbered model 34. The modifications included the deletion of the pressurized cabin and flight engineers station to conserve weight. The defensive armament was changed from the remotely operated system to five manually operated turrets. The twin tail design was substituted for a single vertical stabilizer and finally four bladed Curtis Electric reversible pitch propellers replaced the original three bladed propellers on the XB-32's. The modifications had been ordered because the USAAF was weary about investing identical technologies on two competing aircraft.

Even after the design modifications had been ordered, but not yet tested, the USAAF continued to place orders for the B-32. On 27 January 1944 the second order was for 400 bombers. In addition, there was an order of special tools to be used by maintenance crews. Then on 17 July 1944 the last order was placed for 500 additional aircraft, bringing the grand total to 1,213. The last 500 were to be built at the San Diego plant that had constructed the XB-32's because the B-24 production taking place there was steadily being completed in favor for the B-32.

With each order placed by the USAAF there were requests for replacement parts that were to be shipped to the various testing and training centers using the B-32 and most importantly the combat zone. Consolidated gloated that the replacement parts were being built with the same priority as the actual aircraft. However, this was not actually the case. When the B-32 finally reached the Pacific spare parts were almost nowhere to be found. Some B-32 veterans even questioned if the replacement parts had been erroneously shipped to Europe instead to the Pacific.

When production finally got underway the B-32 was drastically different, left with just proven technologies to safeguard against the failure of the more technologically advanced B-29 Super Fortress, which the B-32 had beaten off the design table and into flight testing back in 1942. However, the B-32 had a significant advancement over the B-29. Four bladed Curtis Electric propellers were on the two inboard engines and, "at the flick of a switch (by the pilot)" the propellers reversed pitch significantly shortening the distance needed for landing to around 2,000 feet and also allowed the it to back up giving the bomber a magnificent ability to maneuver on the ground. One pilot reported that, "It's possible to stop without even touching the breaks."

The redesigned production aircraft retained the cylindrical fuselage that was nine feet six inches in diameter, an overall length of eighty-three feet and one inch and a height of thirty-two feet and two inches. The wingspan remained 135 feet and the engines were upgraded to four 2,200 horse power Wright R-3350-23A's that drove two exhaust driven super chargers on each engine. The propellers were upgraded to Curtis Electric reversible pitch propellers that measured sixteen feet and eight inches, the largest used on any bomber during WWII. The B-32's maximum speed was 330 mph at 10,000 feet and the normal cruising speed was 282 mph at 10,000 feet. To run the engines a maximum of 3,460 gallons of aviation fuel was contained in twelve separate self sealing fuel tanks stored in the center sections of each wing.

The gross weight of the B-32 was 61,000 pounds prior to the installation of combat equipment, when the turret's radio sets and all other required military equipment were added the gross weight increased to 100,000 pounds. 1,622 lbs lighter than the XB-32 model mainly due to the deletion of the remote firing system and the pressurized crew compartments. When the B-32 was fully combat equipped with a 20,000 pound bomb load and a maximum fuel capacity it weighed in at 119,895 pounds, just under maximum weight rating of 125,250 pounds specified by Consolidated.

The new armament on the B-32 consisted of manually operated electric and hydraulic turrets. The Sperry Gyroscope Corporation produced the electric and hydraulically operated A-17 turrets armed with twin .50 caliber machine guns defended the nose and the tail. The nose turret was supplied with 365 rounds of ammunition per gun and was stored outside the turret in ammunition boxes attached to the bulk head between the bombardiers' compartment and the flight deck, the ammunition was fed into the turret by chutes that lead from the ammunition boxes directly into the turret, an arrangement that proved problematic when the B-32 reached combat. The tail was supplied with 1,000 rounds per gun, which was also stored outside in the gunners' compartment. This turret was fed in the same manner as the nose turret. The tail turret was supplied with the most ammunition because attacks on the tail were a favorite of the Japanese.

The positioning of the guns was critical on the Sperry A-17 turrets; they were placed close together allowing the gunner to traverse from right to left as much as possible. Also the placement gave the gunners greater visibility, which was hoped to lead to an increase in accuracy. Another innovation for the turrets allowed the guns to be fired at the same time unlike the ball turret where the fire was staggered which caused the bullets to spread left and right. Robert Nova, an employee of the Sperry, commented on the nose turret position, saying "The view was spectacular, my favorite spot, nothing in front of you but the guns."

Sperry also supplied the hydraulically retractable A-13-A ball turret to protect the underside of the B-32 which was similar to those used on the B-17 and B- 24 bombers. The turret was fully retractable and could rotate 360 degrees. Each of the two M2 .50 caliber machine guns were supplied with 550 rounds, which were stored in ammunition boxes attached to the lowering mechanism of the turret.

The top of the B-32 was defended by two Plexiglas tear drop shaped Martin A-3-0 electric turrets which were also armed with twin .50 caliber machine guns and were supplied with 400 rounds of ammunition each, stored in the turret.

(Above and Below) The front and back of the Sperry A-17 nose and tail turret, when it was owned by the Minnesota Air and Space museum, it was complete out of its original box only missing the M2 Browning .50 caliber machine guns.
(Minnesota Air and Space Museum)

An early B-32 on a demonstration flight over the U.S. (USAAF)

The B-32 had the ability to carry a 20,000 pound bomb load of general purpose or incendiary bombs that were hung on forty eight separate hanging stations. The bomb bay was divided into four separate sections by a beam that served as a catwalk between the forward and aft crew compartments and a structural support divided the bomb bay in half horizontally.

The bomb bay doors rolled up alongside the fuselage of the aircraft, and took just thirteen seconds to open. In addition to bombs, two 1,500 gallon fuel tanks could also be installed in the rear bomb bay giving the Dominator a greater operational range.

The B-32 was intended for an eight man crew consisting of a pilot, co-pilot, bombardier, navigator/nose turret gunner, radio operator and forward top turret gunner, rear top turret gunner, ball turret gunner and tail turret gunner. Later the crew size was increased to ten men when an aerial flight engineer and radar operator were added. The flight engineer was added to the crew because some of the controls were not within easy reach of either the pilot or co-pilot. He was also in

(Above and Below) The first production example (*42-108471*) after completion, it was fitted with a B-29 tail because of stability issues the height tail was later increased. (USAF)

charge of setting and adjusting the autopilot, a useful tool for the long missions in the Pacific. The engineer sat in the opening of the crawl space between the flight deck and the bombardiers' compartment that housed the Norden bomb sight and the nose turret. Often on combat missions the crew sizes ranged from ten to fourteen with the additions of flight instructors, trainees and, at the end of the war, camera operators that also flew as crew members for photographic missions.

The first redesigned B-32, serial number *42-108471*, was not completed until August 1944, due to the design changes enforced by the USAAF. Originally the aircraft was fitted with a sixteen foot tall tail from a B-29 but test flights with the third XB-32 showed stability issues with the shorter tail and prior to the initial test flights by *471* a nineteen and one half foot tall tail replaced the B-29 tail and became one of the B-32's most distinguishing characteristics.

In a Consolidated promotional packet, which was circulated at the end of the war when the B-32 was introduced to the general public, a company representative was quoted saying.

"The B-32 incorporates many outstanding design features making possible longer range and higher speeds with an extra large bomb load."

As production continued flight testing began. Some minor issues with the B-32's lack of vision of the underside of the fuselage and wings were noted. Sight of this area was vital to allow the crew to check for engine fires and anti-aircraft damage. The cockpit noisy and drafty, something a veteran pilot said was nothing worse than any other aircraft he had flown. The B-32 flew at an upward angle of 4 degrees that trapped ninety gallons of fuel in the tanks. Another issue indicated during flight testing was that the aircraft was having a hard time reaching the maximum speed quoted by Consolidated upon completion of their testing.

Another view of *42-108471* after the nineteen and one half foot tall tail was added it was also fitted with a tear drop shaped radar dome. (USAAF via Authors Collection)

The improvements to the B-32 had to be completed during production, directly on the line, as the new planes were built. This was in order to keep up with the production schedule, since innovation was being tested with its production.

Most aircraft built during WWII were completed and flown from their respective manufacturers to modification centers for updating and militarizing, which included arming and adding of military equipment. This was not the case with the B-32, as each bomber was totally completed and equipped ready for delivery to the USAAF as they rolled off the production line.

In the thirteen months of production the majority of the problems found during early test flights were fixed through design modifications incorporated on the production lines. Some of the modifications, along with further design advances, were projected but never accomplished prior to the cancellation of production in June 1945.

This head on view shows the trim lines of the B-32. (USAF)

Even before the B-32 entered combat it was reported by the Associated press on 25 may 1945 that, "Production will be leveled off at the current rate for the remainder of 1945, and will be terminated at the end of the year." The fallowing day USAAF officials remarked that they had opted for the B-29, because of its unexpected performance and low rates of loss. They also decided that only enough B-32's would be produced to meet the demands of crew training and keep it in development.

By the end of the war a total of 118 B-32's, including the three XB-32's and forty TB-32's, were built by Consolidated at their production facilities in Fort Worth and San Diego. In 1944, only fourteen B-32's had been completed and delivered from the Fort Worth plant. A total of 102 had been built and delivered to the USAAF by September of the following year, only one of which was assembled in San Diego. The lone plane's serial number was *44-90486*. The B-32's that were unfinished by the time the contract was cancelled were either completed to a flyable status and flown to storage fields or were simply broken up and scrapped on the production lines.

Another photo of the first production model, this aircraft was used by Consolidated at Fort Worth to test further modifications during the production life of the B-32. (Consolidated via Menge)

The nineteen and one half foot tail on production B-32's gave the bomber an overall height of thirty-two feet. This picture also shows the faring used on TB-32's over the opening for the tail turret. (Consolidated)

CHAPTER 3

DOMINATOR

In December 1944, with XB-32 testing winding down and production still in the early stages, Consolidated had yet to choose a name for their new bomber. On 22 December 1944, the Joint Aircraft Committee formally requested Consolidated submit possible names for the B-32 for approval by the committee.

The goal of the JAC; which was formed by the Navy, Army and British military officials, was to organize a system of naming aircraft. This included aircraft that were a part of the Lend Lease programs. The committee would either choose names for new unnamed aircraft or offer suggestions for changing names of existing aircraft. The guide-lines set by the committee for naming aircraft included that the name could be no longer than one word, it must not have a similar sounding name as any other aircraft and the aircraft must be either in active service or in full production.

To help develop a name, Consolidated hired the advertising agency Young and Rubicam. In a letter from the Consolidated Public Relations Department to the Executive Vice President I. M. Laddon, it is mentioned that the employees in the production plant were calling it the *Crusader,* but found the name had already been registered. A list of fifty-two names was attached to the letter, as seen on page 34.

Annihilator	*Mammoth*	*Deliverance*
Goliath	*Cataclysm*	*Scourger*
Apocalypse	*Monarch*	*Deliverer*
Guardian	*Cavalier*	*Sky Galleon*
Argonaut	*Nemesis*	*Demolisher*
Hercules	*Colossus*	*Sky Terror*
Armageddon	*Olympian*	*Dreadnaught*
Invader	*Commander*	*Steamroller*
Beleaguer	*Overewhelmer*	*Eclipse*
Invincible	*Condor*	*Titan*
Bomb-Toter	*Persuader*	*Earthquaker*
Juggernaut	*Conqueror*	*Triumphant*
Bombwagon	*Redeemer*	*Earthshaker*
Jumbo	*Decimator*	*Vulcan*
Bullbat	*Redemptor*	*Gladiator*
Jupiter	*Decimato*	*Warrior*
Carronade	*Scourge*	*Globe Trotter*

Four were chosen, *Conqueror, Invader, Invincible* and *Titan*. *Invader* was registered by Douglas and was name of their A-26 attack bomber. In a separate letter from Francis Pray, a Technical Writer at Consolidated suggested the name *Emancipator*. This name had been included in the list of fifty two but was ultimately rejected by the JAC.

Eight days later, on 12 January, in a letter to the JAC; Consolidated indicated that they had decided upon the name Terminator. In Response the JAC met on 29 July 1944 and recommended the name be changed to Dominator, at the suggestion of the JAC's Chair Tom M. Girdler. They also gave the name Sea Wolf for the Navy TBY version, even though the Navy had never offered a contract. The names were then approved by the JAC on 3 August 1944. In a letter it is stressed the name should remain restricted until declassified by the USAAF, and asked that the manufacturer look into copyright issues involving the chosen name.

In the summer of 1945 the official name was changed back to Terminator, upon the request of the Assistant Secretary of State Archibald MacLeish. He felt Dominator was "Unbecoming of a U.S. warplane." When the B-32 was finally introduced to the public it was referred to as "The B-32, Super Bomber." Even though the official name was Terminator the moniker never stuck, and to this day the aircraft is still referred to as the B-32 Dominator.

PREPARING FOR WAR

CHAPTER 4

TESTING

When the USAAF originally ordered the B-32 the contract stated the first thirteen aircraft completed were to have the designation YB-32 for use in evaluation of the bombers' capabilities at the different aircraft testing centers around the country. These included Wright Army Air Field in Ohio and Eglin AAF in Florida. However, design changes made prior to production caused the delivery schedule to be delayed. The USAAF, in need of planes, canceled the order for the YB-32's and took the first thirteen modified B-32's as soon as they were available.

The first three modified B-32's came off the production line in the fall of 1944 and were flown at Fort Worth AAF (FWAAF) by USAAF personnel. These three aircraft formed the base of an accelerated test program developed due to the production delays. Consolidated test pilots trained the USAAF pilots who ran the program. The training flights began to take place day and night while production was still in the early stages, when the B-32 was still classified as experimental, to discover any production flaws that needed correcting before major production could begin.

(Above and Below) Two pictures of the second redesigned B-32 (*42-10508472*). It was the first to take flight. Unfortunately it crashed on its maiden flight due to a hydraulic failure. When it landed the landing gear collapsed and the plane was totally destroyed. (USAAF)

42-108480 parked on the tarmac at Eglin AAF between test flights.
(Authors Collection)

The first B-32 that was to be delivered to the USAAF at Wright AAF for evaluation was serial number *42-108472*. It was the first redesigned Dominator to take flight on 19 September 1944, but the plane suffered a hydraulic system failure which caused the main landing gear to collapse upon completion of the test flight, ending its maiden flight in a crash at FWAAF prior to its delivery to Wright AAF.

As the newly designed B-32's began to roll off the assembly line two aircraft serial numbers *42-108473* and *42-108479* were flown to Wright AAF for use in testing which allowed personnel to study the operational specifications on the new design. *479* was used for static testing. *473* was used for flight tests. Eventually *473* was lost when a Lockheed C-60 Constellation crashed into the hanger housing the B-32.

Prior to production the USAAF required the B-32 to be run through one of the most rigorous testing programs required of any aircraft during WWII. The requirements of the test outlined that the

The canvas covers over the turrets and engines were used to keep them warm. Note the B-29 in the background. (Authors Collection)

42-108474 was being evaluated as a test model and was just the fourth aircraft off the assembly line. (Authors Collection)

(Above and Below) Two views of *474* under going regular maintenance between test flights conducted at Fort Worth by the ATSC. (Authors Collection)

minimum of 200 flying hours, the defensive and offensive capabilities needed to be evaluated, along with the Dominator's basic systems. The tests were to be conducted at the Army Air Forces Proving Ground Command (AAFPGC) by the 611th Bomb Squadron (BS) stationed at Eglin AAF. Subsequent tests were conducted by Army Air Forces Tactical Center (AAFTC) at Pinecastle AAF in Florida. A total of seventeen were tested by the Air Tactical Service Command (ATSC) that tested the B-32 at Consolidated, Fort Worth and Wright AAF.

One of the B-32's assigned to the 611th BS at Eglin AAF was piloted by Ken Eidnes, a pilot at the AAFPGC. He recalled what happened while at the controls of what was his first and only B-32 test flight, "The flight lasted an hour and fifty-five minutes, we landed with one engine on fire. I jumped out of the plane as it was rolling to a stop to get as far away as possible." The ground crews had been alerted that

"Laying Eggs," is the caption written on this photograph of the fourteenth aircraft off the production line. *42-108484* was on a practice mission at Eglin AAF. Note the serial number was painted on the underside of the starboard wing between the national insignia and the outboard engine. (Authors Collection)

there was a fire onboard and were standing by. They rushed up to the aircraft as it came to a stop and were able to extinguish the fire before major structural damage took place. Luckily all the crew members were able to escape the fire without injury, except Ken, who had skinned a finger while jumping out.

The B-32 test program proved to be safe and successful overall. There had only been a few minor engine fires and the loss of two Dominators *472* and *42-108475*.

On 10 March 1945 a USAAF test flight crew took *475* up on a routine test flight. When the crew reached 17,000 feet the pilot Capt. Robert Quinn noticed his instruments for the number one and two engines had failed, minutes later the engines followed suit. Immediately Capt. Quinn shut off the power to the number one and two engines and ordered his flight engineer aft to check on the engines. As the flight engineer reached the rear crew compartment he looked out at the left engines and reported to Capt. Quinn over the interphone that there was a fire on the leading edge of the wing burning between the number two engine and the fuselage.

Immediately, the flight engineer attempted twice to extinguish the flames but was unsuccessful in both attempts. When informed that the attempts to extinguish the fire had failed Capt. Quinn then ordered his crew to bail out through the bomb bay and also ordered the flight engineer who was now in the bomb bay to open the bomb bays to allow the crew to escape the stricken bomber, but when the engineer toggled the bomb bay door switch there was no response. He immediately went back to the flight deck and informed Capt. Quinn of the malfunctioning bomb bay doors. He was then ordered to manually open the bomb bay doors. Just as he reached the passage way from the flight deck to the bomb bay flames poured through the passage way and into the flight deck, starting the cloth sound insulation that lined the interior of the flight deck on fire.

Meanwhile the three crew members in the rear crew compartment received their order to bail out. Unable to escape through the bomb bay the three opted for the camera hatch that was on the floor in the rear crew compartment and were forced to bail out through flames that were streaking down the fuselage of *475*. Each of the three received severe burns as they exited the bomber.

On the flight deck the remaining crew members were forced to abandon the stricken Dominator through the bombardiers hatch due to the inferno ragging through the interior of the bomber. Capt. Quinn was eventually the last man out being chased by the flames as he exited and *475* plummeted to the ground below.

By 1 August 1945 sixty B-32's were being used to train crews in the U.S. and only three were in active combat. Those not used for combat or training were used for testing. During the test program maintenance crews found the B-32 an enjoyable aircraft with a stable bombing platform and felt it was easy to work on, with the majority of

42-108476 was another of the Dominators assigned to Eglin AAF in late 1944 and conducted services test up until the end of the war. The large number "6" painted on the tail was its field identification number. (USAAF)

key equipment easily accessible. The crews did voice that the flight deck was quite noisy on the early models. Flight testing continued throughout the duration of the war and was finally ordered to stop in October 1945.

CHAPTER 5

TRAINING

The story of the B-32 crew training program is an important portion of the bomber's history. More B-32's were used for training than ever reached the combat zone. Not one crew that was trained at any of the AAF training centers throughout the country ever flew a B-32 combat mission.

When the USAAF placed its order for the forty TB-32's in 1944 a new milestone was reached in how bomber crews would be trained. The TB-32 was the first bomber modified to serve exclusively as a tactical training aircraft. All defensive armament had been left off during assembly and covered over with metal fairings. The tactical equipment, such as radio, was kept to a minimum along with the deletion of radar. To make up for the lost weight in the defensive armament and tactical equipment 700 lbs of ballast weight was added to the rear section of the aircraft during assembly.

The role of the TB-32 was to serve as a transition aircraft for veteran and newly trained B-24 pilots and crew members that formed the core of the B-32 trainee pool. Arriving along with the new aircraft came a new way of training for the USAAF. The 2159th Army Air Force Base Unit (AAFBU) at FWAAF (formally Tarrent AAF) was

49

a B-24 training facility prior to the arrival of the Dominator and was chosen as the main B-32 training center. This was an obvious decision because Fort Worth, AAF just happened to share an airstrip with the Consolidated Aircraft Corporations plant producing the new bombers.

Planning for the training program had begun as early as fall 1944. Flying and maintenance schedules were created as well as an outline for the training program, which was organized to be innovative and all inclusive. The goal of the training program was to provide experienced crews in as short a time possible. Since there was a lack of TB-32's, modified B-24's were used to assimilate the crews to some of the new systems that had been added to the B-24's to resemble the B-32. All the necessary training except for the gunners, radar operators, navigators and bombardiers was to be conducted at FWAAF. The initial crews consisted of veteran B-24 pilots.

Crews were trained by Consolidated test pilots and the flight crews who were trained by those same test pilots in order to evaluate the B-32 at Wright AAF. Upon completion of their training they form-

A head on view of a TB-32, a B-29 is directly behind it. (Authors Collection)

A factory fresh TB-32 on a test flight up among the high cumulus. (USAAF)

ed the core of the instructors that would train crews at Fort Worth and eventually other B-32 training centers such as Mountain Home AAF in Idaho and Walnut Ridge AAF in Arkansas.

The first training programs organized were for the maintenance personnel and flight engineers and took place at Keesler AAF in Mississippi, Chunalte AAF in Illinois and at Consolidated's plant in San Diego. The men chosen for the maintenance crews were all former line chiefs, all of which had previous experience working on four engine aircraft. The first three flight engineers MSgt. Clyde Sharrer, MSgt. Emil Gabrys and MSgt. William H. Gauthier, were sent to Consolidated's San Diego plant to be trained by company officials in a specific aerial engineer training program. The maintenance personnel were sent across the runways to the Consolidated Fort Worth plant for their initial training to learn the aircrafts systems as they were being assembled be cause of the production delays. Early training programs at

Keesler AAF were hampered by a lack of available teaching aids, technical manuals and aircraft.

The first TB-32's were scheduled for delivery in April 1945. FWAAF required some expansion before the arrival of the Dominators to support the larger and heavier aircraft. The runways were widened and lengthened and the aprons where the aircraft were parked and repaired required enlarging and re-enforcing to support the weight of the B-32. Along with the improvements to the airstrip and apron two new large hangers were built and more classrooms were added to support the larger classes that were required for the massive training effort.

The first TB-32 assigned to 2159th AAFBU was serial number, *42-108489*. The Dominator was taxied across the runways from the Consolidated plant during the afternoon of 27 January 1945. The commanding officer of FWAAF, Col. H.W. Door and his staff welcomed their first TB-32 with minor fanfare, as the entire B-32 program was still confidential. Upon the arrival of the first Dominator a large number "1" was painted on the aircraft just under the cockpit on the co-pilots side.

In February 1945 the training program at FWAAF began and was starting to pick up in pace with the arrival of new TB-32's as they came off the assembly line. As crew training began, the 4th Air Force was transferred to FWAAF. The 4th AF was originally a B-24 group preparing to leave for the European theater until they were recalled to begin training as the proposed first all B-32 Bomb Group.

One of the veteran B-24 pilots trained at FWAAF was Wayne G. Grooms, who had flown B-24's in Europe. Upon his return to the States in August of 1944 he was assigned to the 426th AAFBU at Mountain Home AAF as a senior B-24 instructor. In late March of 1945 he was ordered to FWAAF to receive training as a B-32 flight instructor. "The aircraft we flew in training were without turrets, or any extras." On training missions, "The crew consisted of a senior B-32 instructor pilot and two student pilots and, of course, a flight engineer. On a training mission you were required to demonstrate your knowledge of all the aircrafts systems and emergency procedures," He recalled about his days spent training at FWAAF.

Starting up! OM-12 was one of the TB-32's stationed at FWAAF. Each aircraft was given an identification code that was painted on both sides of the fuselage, and replicated on the tail and the faring over the tail turret. (USAAF)

After a month of training he was sent back to Mountain Home AAF in early May 1945. Wayne then became a flight instructor in the B-32 training program that was scheduled to begin by the end of May. The first B-32 was assigned on 26 May 1945 and by June only five B-32's had been assigned. After completing just two training flights by June, he was informed he had accumulated enough points to be discharged and was ordered to Fort Douglas, Utah for discharge. "I thoroughly enjoyed flying that aircraft, it had plenty of power for its weight and was very responsive to the controls," he recalled about his B-32 flying days. Also at the end of June the five B-32's assigned to the 426th AAFBU were reassigned to FWAAF canceling B-32 training at Mountain Home AAF.

The training of B-32 crews was broken into a two month process. The first month of training the, pilots, co-pilots and flight engineers trained together in TB-32's. The first two weeks were spent in the classroom learning the interior and exterior of the new bomber. The airplane commander, or first pilot, was in charge of the crew, the aircraft, and were required to know everything about the operation of it.

The copilot was an assistant to the airplane commander and was required to know the same things as though he was the aircraft's commander. The last member of the crew, the aerial engineer had a highly important job for an enlisted man. He was expected to supply the pilots with in flight data and setting the controls for the "cruise control" or autopilot. The third and fourth weeks were spent in the aircraft. The crews were required to complete a seventy item pre-flight check list before taking off. Once airborne they flew, as they put it, a series of "Circuits and bumps," consisting of a series of takeoffs, following the traffic pattern, and landings in continuous successions. The pilots were required to fly a total of fifty hours and copilots were required to fly twenty five hours as observers and a second twenty five hours flying the bomber.

The open bomb bay doors of this TB-32 show how the bomb bay was divided into four sections. The B-32 could carry a 20,000 lb bomb load. (USAF)

Formation flying was just one of the many skills pilots were required to master while training at FWAAF. (USAAF via Authors Collection)

Meanwhile, the bombardiers, navigators and radar operators were trained simultaneously for the first month at other training facilities specific to their specialty. The gunners were trained at Laredo AAF, due to the fact that there was not a gunnery range at FWAAF and the crews were flying the unarmed TB-32. A special gunnery school had been organized for the sole purpose of training the gunners on the new Sperry A-17 nose and tail turrets and the other B-32 turrets.

Among the gunners who trained at Laredo AAF was Roger Arendsee. Roger was a gunner aboard a B-24 stationed in Italy with the 513th BS prior to his returning home. Upon his arrival, he was given orders to report to Laredo AAF to become an instructor. He learned the operation of the turrets, especially the nose and tail turrets. "We had been told that the B-32 was behind in production, and they had doubts as to whether remote control turrets would really work, they decided to redesign the B-32 using occupied gyro controlled turrets just to be sure they had a reliable gunnery system. That put the B-32 behind schedule." With his training completed Roger received orders to report to Yuma, Arizona to organize a second gunnery school. Upon their arrival the instructors were informed that the base had never received any turrets or an actual B-32. Roger and the other gunners decided to remain in Yuma and spent the last months of the war stationed there.

Upon the completion of the first month of training the separate groups began their second month of training as a combined flight crew. The second month's training required a total of eighty flying hours; the first forty were flown in TB-32's and the last forty in fully combat equipped B-32's. When the crews completed their second month of training they were supposed to be sent to the Pacific to take part in combat operations. Unfortunately, not a single flight crew with formal B-32 training from FWAAF was every transferred to the Pacific to take part in the B-32's short lived combat career.

Among the pilots to train at FWAAF was a fully qualified B-24 pilot named Robert Kirk. On the day he and his crew were to deploy to China and fly B-24's against Japan they were transferred to 2159th AAFBU to join the B-32 training program.

When they arrived at FWAAF the crew was immediately awe struck by the B-32. "The first thing that struck all of us was the size of the B-32 in comparison to the B-24. The next thing was the spaciousness of the flight deck. It was like a small room compared to the flight deck of the B-24. The navigator had a drop down table of a size he could spread out his charts."

For Robert Kirk the transition training was smooth, except for the fact that an entirely new take off procedure had to be learned. During flight, in order to gain altitude, the pilots would climb fifty to one hundred feet upon take off, then level off and repeat the procedure until reaching their desired altitudes. This tactic made take offs to the north a bit interesting. At the north end of the airfield was Lake Worth and on the other side of the lake was a steep hill with homes on top. With the gradual climb the B-32's just cleared the homes at roof top level, "This was not appreciated by the people with residences on top of the hill," recalled Robert.

TB-32 *42-108522* being flown on an early test flight after its completion at the Fort Worth production facility, upon completion of the flight it was delivered to the USAAF and accepted by the 2159th AFGBU. (USAAF via Authors Collection)

He found the B-32 easier to fly than the B-24, "The controls were smoother and more responsive. To me it was like flying a B-25. I always felt the B-32 was a more forgiving aircraft. This was not to say you could fly along making a series of errors but the B-24 was quick to try and get the upper hand in any situation. I had only one what I would consider a real emergency in a B-32 but I believe I was able to get out of with less difficulty than if I would have had the same problem in the B-24."

During some of his training flights Navy F6F Hellcats from Naval Air Station Dallas would join in formation with the B-32's. "I found the airspeed of a B-32 quite surprising." When the Hellcats joined in formation they could do so without having to lower their flaps to slow down with the B-32. Robert's training continued and he became more and more impressed with the B-32. He summed up his overall impressions of the Dominator as, "A superior aircraft which came on the scene too late to be affective. It weighed loaded what a B-29 weighed empty, with the same Davis wing design and the Wright engines the B-32 could have flown missions with a heavier bomb load for greater effective range than the B-29."

The training program at FWAAF showed the B-32's reliability. In more than 8,500 hours of flying time there had been only one accident prior to 1 August 1945. The crew led by instructor and airplane commander Lt. M.G. Alderfer onboard TB-32, *42-108495* experienced a fire as the crew was running a series of circuits. On their seventh takeoff the crewmen reported smelling smoke but were unable to find the source. Lt. Alderfer took control of the Dominator taking it out of the traffic pattern and climbed to check for the source of the fire. When they reached 5,000 feet the co-pilot reported to Lt. Alderfer that flames were streaming from the number three engine, immediately Lt. Alderfer cut power to the engine and feathered the prop. The crew tried in vain to extinguish the fire. Finally, Lt. Alderfer ordered the crew to bail out, he stayed with the plane for a short while longer trying to extinguish the fire but soon followed his crew out through the bomb bay. The pilot-less plane spiraled to the ground with the right wing in flames and crashed.

One of the crew members on board *495* was Sgt. Harold Keller who was reported in the official paper of FWAAF, *The Tarranteer,* saying, "If my ripcord had been welded in, that jerk I gave it would have got it out. I told my girlfriend not to ever complain again about rayon stockings. That nylon chute over me looked better right there then on any woman's legs." The paper concluded its report with, "No one was injured and the eight crew members made successful emergency jumps and took their regular turn at training the next day.

The B-32 remained a secret until Air Force Day which was 1 August 1945 and FWAAF was chosen to host an event that formally introduced the public to the Dominator that had been flying over the city and surrounding area since late 1944. A day of activities was focused around the B-32 which included a fly over of B-32's in formation with P-38 Lightning's twice during the day. The public was also shown the highlights of the field and the B-32 training program in the day long events.

Three TB-32's in formation on a demonstration flight over Texas. (USAAF)

Crew training was completed by October 1945. A total of 240 pilots and copilots were trained and another 140 officers and non commissioned officer were trained, including navigators, gunners and flight engineers.

THE B-32 GOES TO WAR

CHAPTER 6

"THE COOK PROJECT"

By the fall of 1944 every bomber command in the Pacific wanted the B-29, but no one was requesting the B-32. One of the men clambering for the B-29 was the Commanding General of the 5th Air Force (AF) of the Far Eastern Air Force (FEAF) General George Kenney. After receiving several refusals to his request, Gen. Kenney flew to Washington D.C. in March 1945 to meet with Gen. H. H. Arnold. It was during this trip that Kenney became the first officer to formally request the B-32. After a close up inspection of two fully equipped combat B-32's, which had been flown to Washington for closer inspections and a demonstration flight, Gen. Kenny requested the B-32, offering thorough testing in combat to prove their effectiveness. Gen. Arnold contemplated the offer and, on 25 March 1945, he agreed to equip one squadron with B-32's for a combat test. If the B-32 passed the test more Dominators would be sent to accompany those already in the field. However, if the B-32 failed then production was to be formally cancelled.

Rumors began to circulate in early May 1945, among the men of the 312th Bomb Group (BG) that there was to be a change in aircraft. The rumors proved right, as Gen. Kenny chose the 386th BS of 312th

BG to be the first squadron equipped with the new "Super Bomber." The officer chosen to administrate the combat test was an officer that had never flown a combat mission but was an experienced test pilot, Col. Frank R. Cook. Col. Cook was well known in USAAF for flying the first B-29, *Hobo Queen* to Europe and then onto China over German territory. At the time of his appointment to head the combat test, he was a pilot with the ATSC and from that moment the test was referred to as "The Cook Project."

The men chosen to be the first B-32 combat crews were not taken from the training program at FWAAF, but were selected from different aircraft testing fields throughout the country. On 1 May 1945, the men assigned to the "Cook Project" gathered across the runways from the B-32 training program at FWAAF at Consolidated's plant to begin flight training and familiarizing themselves to the B-32, whose fate they held in their hands.

Just twelve days later, 12 May 1945 two B-32's, serial numbers *42-108529* and *42-108532* which was led by Col. Cook, left FWAAF for Mather AAF in California. It was the first stop on their journey to Clark Field, on the Philippine island of Luzon, to begin combat testing. The crews landed at Mather AAF without incident and were processed for their trip, and their bombers were checked over.

On 14 May 1945, another B-32, *42-108528* left FWAAF to join *529* and *532* at Mather AAF. *528* was not originally intended for the combat test, but joined the project due to a landing gear issue suffered by the plane originally picked *42-108531*. *528* was fresh off the assembly line and had not received the desired amount of test flights to check for flaws prior to its deployment, an oversight that proved to be a mistake as *528* began its troublesome journey into the war.

The trouble began upon their arrival at Mather AAF. While making their final approach to the airfield the co-pilot onboard attempted to lower the landing gear but there was no response, so the crew was forced to lower the landing gear manually, which was an exhausting and cumbersome feat that allowed them to land safely. Upon inspection by maintenance crews the generator powered by the number two engine was found to be faulty but was not replaced, in order to preserve the few spare parts that each aircraft was carrying along to the combat zone.

Two days later, on 16 May, the work on *528* was still in progress when Col. Cook decided not to wait any longer for *528* and told the crews of *529* and *532* that they would depart for the second leg of their journey at 0115 heading for Honolulu ahead of *528*. Their flight was uneventful and lasted roughly twelve hours and ten minutes. The following day *528* was finally ready, and left for Honolulu through a thick cloud cover.

Unfortunately, the string of bad luck continued during this flight when the crew became lost, flying 260 miles off course. The navigator was then forced to use the sun to guide them back on course.

By 17 May the three B-32's were together again. While in Hawaii *528* and *529* required some minor repairs, including an engine change for *529* which was completed on 19 May. The original route that the B-32's were to take to Clark Field had them flying from Honolulu to New Guinea, then north to the Philippines. This was changed when the Dominators reached Hawaii. The new route took them to first to Kwajalein, then to Guam, and finally to Clark Field, a route which, while there were more stops, was more direct.

528 still required a test flight before heading out over the vast Pacific when Col. Cook, again anxious to get things started, decided to leave without *528*. So once again *529* and *532* moved on, heading for Kwajalein to be refueled, and then flying seven hours more to Guam. *528*, which left Honolulu on 21 May finally reached Kwajalein on 22 May, was refueled and prepared to leave for Guam. Once again, electrical problems, which would need repair, caused them to extend their stay. The plane finally reached Guam on 24 May.

While the crews of the B-32's were at Guam they were able to briefly rest and meet the curious B-29 crews that had been flying missions against Japan for nearly a year. The crewmen gathered to check out the USAAF's "other" Very Heavy bomber.

When the time came for the Dominators to depart on 24 May the wreckage of a crashed B-29 blocked the end of the runway. Col. Cook opted to show off the abilities of the B-32, which needed a much shorter distance for take off than the B-29. He headed down the run way and lifted *532* up over the wreckage, with *529* close behind, much to the astonishment of the men stationed at Guam.

The Lady is Fresh upon arrival at Clark Field. (USAF)

Finally, on 24 May 1945 the rumors that had passed through the 312th BG earlier in the month came to fruition with the arrival at Clark Field of *529,* now known as *The Lady is Fresh,* and *532,* named *Hobo Queen II,* after the first B-29 he flew to Europe, *Hobo Queen.* When they arrived, Col. Cook pulled *Hobo Queen II* directly up to the base operations building and climbed out. The startled officers inside, ran outside, screaming there was not enough room to turn the bomber around.

Col. Cook proceeded to climb back aboard and, with a loud roar from the engines as the pitch of the inboard propellers were reversed; he backed up *Hobo Queen II,* much to the amazement of his audience. The following day *528,* which was never given an unofficial name by its crew, finally joined the other B-32's in the Philippines.

Arriving along with Dominators were USAAF personnel, including trained flight engineers and maintenance crew chiefs. There were also ten civilians from Consolidated and the different manufacturers that built portions of the bomber, including the Sperry Gyro Scope Corporation that built the nose and tail turrets. The civilians had been instructed prior to their departure that they were to organize a training school to help transition crews to the new B-32's. However the USAAF had never intended them to do this, expecting the crews that had ferried the B-32's from Fort Worth to organize a training program and to use the civilians as advisors when training got underway a week later.

The preparations for the training of combat and ground crews were abruptly placed on hold as the Dominators were prepared for their first attack on the Japanese. This brought them into the heart of the battle on Luzon, and ordered them to bomb a well-defended Japanese position.

29 May 1945

The first ever B-32 combat mission was not originally a part of the required combat test program, nor was it even recognized as the first official mission by the USAAF. On the morning of 29 May 1945, the crews that ferried the Dominators to Clark Field were assembled and briefed for their first mission. They were informed by Col. Cook that their target was a Japanese supply depot, located in the Northern Luzon town of Antatet in the Cayagan Valley. The position was guarded by a garrison of approximately fifty men and one general officer, who were armed with several 75 mm guns, slowing the advance of Philippine guerrillas who were trying to capture it.

Each crew consisted of ten men, plus three observers per Dominator. During their preflight briefing the crews were instructed to make three passes over the target. The first was to identify the target by locating a large warehouse with a new metal roof and another warehouse being constructed just to the east in the south west corner of the town. On the second pass the crews were to fly over the target individually, dropping their payloads of nine, 1,000 lb bombs on the town. With the conclusion of the bomb run a third and final pass was to be conducted to photograph the results of the mission.

At 1030 *Hobo Queen II*, *The Lady is Fresh* and *528* began leaving Clark Field. The crew of *528*, anxious to get into the thick of things, believed their mechanical woes were behind them and started their take off run. A third of the way down the runway a super charger failed, jerking the bomber to one side, almost pulling it off of the edge of the runway. Luckily, tragedy was avoided when the pilot was able to regain control but *528*, but was forced to abort the mission. *Hobo Queen II* and *The Lady is Fresh* had already taken off and continued on without *528*.

They headed east from Clark Field and the two Dominators rallied over Baler Bay and their gunners test fired their guns. During testing, the nose turret on *Hobo Queen II* jammed; the turret was catching on the ammunition chutes that fed ammunition to the turret from the ammunition boxes stored in the bombardier's compartment. However this did not deter the crews from carrying on with the mission and the B-32's turned north for the 190 mile flight to the target.

The Dominators arrived at Antatet and made their initial pass, taking the required pre-strike photographs and positively identifying the target. At 1200 *The Lady is Fresh* pilots by Col. Kendall Paul, flew over the target at an altitude of 10,000 feet and dropped its nine 1,000 lbs bombs on the northern potion of the target. *Hobo Queen II*, piloted by Col. Cook, followed from the south east dropping its bombs on the southern portion of Antatet. The crew onboard *Hobo Queen II* observed their bombs exploding amongst the buildings in the town damaging the warehouse with the new metal roof.

A final pass was made over the target to take the required post strike photographs. Then the crews turned for home. They experienced no resistance over the target, and made their triumphant return to Clark Field at 1350, completing the two hour and thirty five minute mission.

According the Japanese the mission on 29 May was not the first B-32 mission. The fallowing day 30 May, Japanese officials released a press release stating, "The American's had thrown their new B-34 Super Liberator bomber into action against Japan." They continued stating that the B-34 was a larger Liberator, and that it appeared over the southern Japanese Island of Honshu and it had been shot down. In response the Associated Press reporter stated, "There is no B-34 Super Liberator, but there is a B-32 in production, but has not been official announced in action."

The "Roarin' 20's" sign outside of Floridablanca, the 312th BG comprised of the 386th, 387th, 388th and 389th BS's. All four squadrons were to be equipped with Dominators. (Authors Collection)

On 31 May 1945, after a week at Clark Field, the B-32's of the "Cook Project" were transferred to Floridablanca Airfield, twenty five miles southeast of Clark Field and were officially assigned to the 386th BS. Floridablanca was originally intended as a B-29 base, but B-29's were never assigned to the Philippines. The airstrip became home to the "Cook Project" and what would become the "B-32 school", as named in the official records of the 312th BG.

On 1 June 1945, Brigadier General J.V. Crabb, Commander of V Bomber Command, presented an outline for the combat test that was scheduled to last until the end of June. Outlined in the report were the three major aspects to be evaluated. The first covered engineering, specifically bomb loading, aeronautics, formation flying, handling of the aircraft under emergency situations and the positioning of equipment throughout the aircraft for possible design modifications. The second covered the maintenance of the bombers. The information gathered was necessary to inform future maintenance personnel and the Air Services Command of the amount of time required to prepare an aircraft between missions. The total flying hours flown by each B-32 were also required in this section; along with the availability of spare parts, the adequacy of maintenance facilities and the training of maintenance personnel.

The final section outlined the Combat Test in strict detail. V Bomber Command assigned ten missions, and guidelines for each mission which included location, altitude, fuel amounts, bomb load and method of bombing to be used (visual or radar). Also the offensive and defensive capabilities were to be evaluated and critiqued in the final report. To assist in the evaluation process photographs of the target were required to be taken before, during and after each mission to determine the level of effectiveness.

When the company advisors and the crews that ferried the B-32's to the Pacific arrived at Floridablanca they began to organizing the "B-32 School." The courses were held in tents and covered the bombsights, radios, radar (which was new to most of the crews), navigation, the powered turrets and maintenance.

On 2 June, after the outline for the combat trail was issued, Col. Cook asked the civilian advisors to become instructors to assist the USAAF personnel in the transition training.

Robert Nova, an employee of Sperry, was one of the civilian instructors. His job was to instruct the gunners on the workings of the new gun turrets, computer gun sights, bore sighting the guns, and everything else pertaining to the functioning of the turret. He recalled that, "The gunners slept through most of my classes because they were pros with the .50 caliber machine gun and knew it like the backs of their hands."

The transition crews consisted mainly of B-24 pilots and flights crews from the 19th, 22nd, 43rd and 380th BG's stationed in the Pacific theater and a select few of A-20 crewmen from the four squadrons of the 312th BG. The majority of the crews assigned to the 386th BS were transferred to the remaining units in the 312th BG still flying A-20's, or were offered transfers to other bomb groups. The maintenance personnel were drawn from V Bomber Command and replacement centers, with an emphasis placed on men with prior four engine experience.

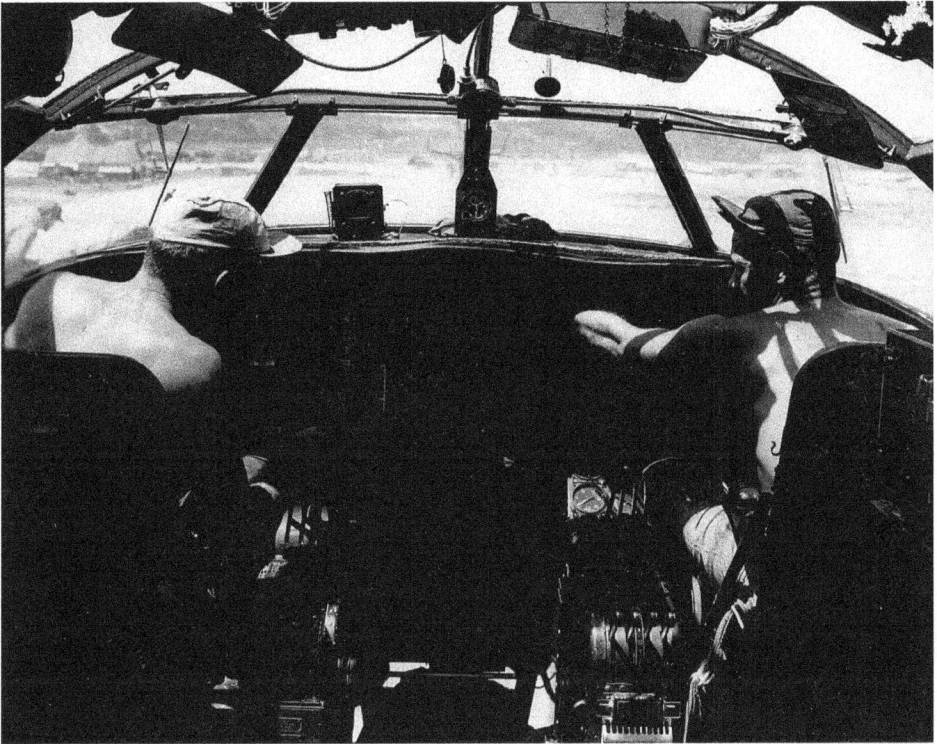

Two "Cook Project" GI's going over the controls on the instrument panel. In the space between the two control pedestals is the passage way to the nose compartment, where the flight engineer sat during missions. (Authors collection)

Among the first crews to be trained in the B-32 school were former A-20 gunners (John) Jack Munsell, who was assigned to the B-32 program to become a flight engineer, and SSgt Julius "Julie" A. Kossor, who had been a member of the 389th BS before transferring to the 386th BS for transition training.

Jack Munsell had bounced around in his short career in the USAAF. He began training to become a pilot but, because of a vision problem, was transferred to B-17 maintenance training and then to Douglas A-20 factory school, and then transferred to aerial gunnery school on B-24's, finally returning to A-20 crew training. Shortly after arriving in the Philippines with the 387th BS he was told to pack his

71

things again and was transferred to the 386th BS for his B-32 training. "There were five or six of us scheduled to switch from light bombers to very heavy bombers," Recalled Jack Munsell.

"We were taught by former flight engineers who had completed combat tours on B-17's and B-24's and were on detached duty from the States," he said. The school had been set up in tents to keep them closed off. The classroom portion of the training lasted for two weeks and included ground training and some flight training. "Our instructors commenced checking us out as B-32 flight engineers and gunners. I was checked out after my second flight, all of us had graduated from gunnery school and were familiar with the Sperry and Martin turrets," he continued.

SSgt. Julie Kossor had turned down a transfer to another squadron that would have kept him with his A-20 crew, which had been transferred to a Squadron flying B-25's, simply because he didn't want to fly on B-25's. Julie was assigned to the 386th BS and became a ball

Hobo Queen II, the original nose art painted on *532*. (noseartphotos.com)

turret gunner. During his time in the Pacific he kept a journal that offers a glimpse into the transition training and the combat life of the B-32. He flew his last A-20 mission on 3 June 1945, and wrote in his journal, "Glad it was my last mission in A-20's. Really had some close calls these last few missions and will now fly on B-32's!"

In a journal entry for 6 June 1945 he wrote about his first encounter with the B-32. "Assigned to one of three planes in entire group for shakedown crews and test, ship has a lot of bugs. Had to change one engine and then it caught fire, as we were about to taxi out and take off. We got out but fast and finally after four days, we got to fly in it, test fired the guns and had a good ride. Ball in bad condition and had to fix many parts." The first mission of the combat test would take place just two days later.

The officers trained alongside the enlisted men in the B-32 school. Col. F.L. Svore was a Captain at the time with the 386th BS and had flown over eighty missions in A-20's and B-25's. After the arrival of the B-32's, Capt. Svore was named Unit Commander, recalling, "I shot two landings in the B-32 and was "checked out" and promoted to Commander and I also had no apprehensions about switching to the four engine high altitude bomber from the low level twin engine attack aircraft." The transition was easier due to the well-trained flight engineers that arrived along with the Dominators. "They gave a pilot a great deal of confidence and made a huge difference in the ease of transitioning the new B-32 pilots," said Col. Svore.

Col. Cook had been chosen to head the combat test even though he lacked prior combat experience, "He was determined to fly missions, he was very receptive to guidance, suggestions and he let combat experienced pilots often lead," remembered Col. Svore. Due to this Capt. Svore was designated as the aircraft commander/pilot on board the lead B-32 on each combat mission and on single aircraft missions he was to command the lone aircraft. Eventually, this wasn't always the case, and he led around ten missions. Capt. Svore's other duties as Squadron Commander had him administrating the day-to-day operations of the 386th BS and working closely with Col. Cook in planning each mission.

The majority of "The Cook Project's" missions were to the island of Formosa, current day Taiwan. The Japanese had stationed large quantities of men and material on the island which was never invaded, even though Admiral Chester Nimitz pushed for it as an alternative to the invasion of the Philippines, leaving the island to become a virtual bomb range to hold the troops and supplies in place. Assigned to fly in support of the B-32's on some missions were A-20's, B-25's and B-24's that were used to finish off the targets that B-32's had softened up.

By the first week of June, the transition training program had a total of 163 flyers in the B-32 School. The first couple of missions were designed to help the crews adjust to the new B-32's, explained Jack Munsell, "We flew four or five missions (not all combat missions) to northern Luzon to familiarize the crews with the B-32's equipment and locations before flying missions to Formosa and China."

The transitioning for the radar operators, turret gunners, and communications personnel had been scheduled to be completed by 23 June 1945 and the training for maintenance personnel and ground crews continued throughout the duration of the combat evaluation.

12 June 1945

The mission on 12 June was officially the first mission of the combat test. During the pre-flight briefing the crews were informed that their target was the Basco aerodrome located on the island of Bataan. The crews had also learned that there had been little to no opposition on previous missions to the airstrip and the same should be expected on this mission. Due to this, Col. Cook and Capt. Svore planned for each bomber to make two individual runs over the target so the effectiveness of the Dominator could be better judged.

The crews, consisting of fifteen officers and enlisted men, climbed aboard *The Lady is Fresh* and *Hobo Queen II*. Unfortunately, *528* was in need of an engine change and was left behind at Florida-blanca. Each Dominator was loaded with forty 500 lb bombs and 3,350 gal of fuel for the mission. At 0930 *Hobo Queen II* was the first to leave followed by *The Lady is Fresh* a few minutes later. They flew to Lingayen Gulf and from there flew along the west coast of Luzon to

Bataan. Upon their arrival over the target a pass was made by *Hobo Queen II* to photograph the aerodrome and the crews on board reported that the strip was, "Rough but serviceable."

At 1117, rumbling in from the southwest, *Hobo Queen II* arrived over the target for a second time to make a "delivery" to the Japanese below. From an altitude of 16,000 ft, the bombardier focused his bombsite on the airstrip and released ten of his twenty bombs. The crew watched as the bombs exploded on the center of the runway and spread towards the north end of the strip, a direct hit! *Hobo Queen II* flew around again to make its second bomb run over the target from the same direction. Over the airstrip the last ten bombs in the bomb bay were released and fell in almost the same place as those on the previous run.

As *Hobo Queen II* was leaving the target area *The Lady is Fresh* made its first bomb run approaching the target from the northwest. From an altitude of 15,500 ft the crew watched as its first ten bombs

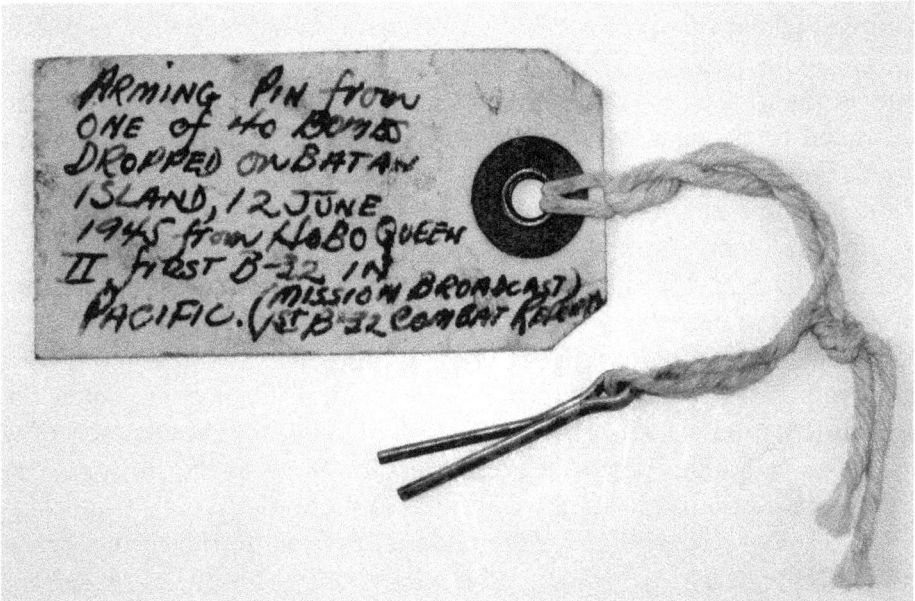

One of twenty arming pins from the bombs dropped by *Hobo Queen II* on 12 June 1945, the pin states it is from the first B-32 mission. (Authors collection)

75

fell on the field and five of the bombs exploded on the east center of the airstrip. Then at 1138 *The Lady is Fresh* made its second run, this time from the west. The final ten 500 lb bombs exploded on the northern end of the runway and the Dominators turned for home following the same route in which they had come.

They arrived back at Floridablanca at 1330 and the crews in their post flight briefing reported to the squadron's intelligence officers that the airstrip was, "Definitely unserviceable." After the mission, as maintenance crews were checking over the bombers, a hole was found in the left horizontal stabilizer of *The Lady is Fresh*. The crews got excited because the hole was the diameter of a .50 caliber machine gun round, but was later determined to have been caused not by a bullet but a bomb fragment from a previous low level practice mission.

13 June 1945

The target for 13 June was the Koshun aerodrome on the occupied island of Formosa. Each Dominator was loaded the previous evening with twelve 1,000 lb bombs and 4,000 gal of fuel for a 480 mile flight to the target. This was the first mission the B-32's were scheduled to fly against Japanese strongholds on Formosa. The crews of ten, plus four trainees and an observer, climbed aboard *Hobo Queen II* and *528*, onboard *528* was Julie Kossor on his first B-32 mission.

The Dominators left Floridablanca at 0800 and headed north to Formosa. During the three hour flight to the target Julie Kossor slept away the time on a bunk located between the tail turret compartment and the rear crew compartment. At an altitude of 12,000 ft *Hobo Queen II* arrived over the target at 1100. Through significant cloud cover the bombardier released all twelve of his bombs and the crew watched as nine of their bombs exploded on the leading edge of the runway with the last three bombs hitting the west side of the runway.

Fifteen minutes later, *528* made its first bomb run of the war at 1115. As they flew over the target the bombardier hit the bomb release switch to drop all twelve bombs but only nine fell to the target exploding on the center of the southern portion of the airstrip. Julie Kossor wrote in his journal that "He had a perfect view of the target," from the ball turret and observed "Three bombs made direct hits on the runway and the others fell all around the field." As *528* pulled away from the target three 1,000 pounders were hung up in the bomb bay. As they headed south away from the target the remaining bombs were salvoed off the southern cost of Formosa and the crews headed for home.

The crews returned to Floridablanca unscathed at 1425 from their first mission to Formosa. *The Lady is Fresh* had stayed behind because of repairs that were being made on the damaged left horizontal stabilizer.

15 June 1945

On 14 June maintenance crews began work equipping the Dominators with type E-2 inflatable life rafts that were stored in compartments on the outer fuselage. These life rafts were to be used if the crews were forced to ditch in the ocean miles from a possible rescue. The work was complex, each raft had to be carefully packed and the emergency inflate lines had to be run from the storage compartments into the flight deck and the rear crew compartment. It is interesting that the work wasn't completed prior to their departure because the official history of the 386th BS states that it was necessary maintenance due to the missions to Formosa, which required them to fly over water for long durations of time. By the following morning *528* was still being equipped with the life rafts, leaving just *The Lady is Fresh* and *Hobo Queen II* available for the next mission.

The following morning the crews of *The Lady is Fresh* and *Hobo Queen II*, consisting of ten plus four trainees per bomber and an observer, were informed of their target, a sugar mill located at Tiato Town, on the east coast of Formosa. The Japanese were refining alcohol made from sugar cane into butanol for use as aviation fuel. This was an essential part of the Japanese war effort due to the dwindling supply of fossil fuels available to them by this stage of the war.

Capt. Svore was directed by Col. Cook to lead the mission which began at 0800 when he lifted *The Lady is Fresh* off of the Floridablanca runway and headed for Formosa via the west coast of Luzon. Each Dominator was loaded the previous day with eight 2,000 lb bombs for the mission and while in route to the target the crews observed a moderate cloud cover at 5,000 to 6,500 ft. As they arrived over the target Col. Svore decided that they would approach the target from the sea hoping to avoid a weather system that was forming over the mountains on the western side of Formosa.

Hobo Queen II was the first over the target, at 1138. It approached from the southeast and at an altitude of 15, 000 ft all eight of their bombs were released. However, all of the bombs fell well off target, landing in a river bed 2,000 ft northeast of the target. Now it was the turn of *The Lady is Fresh*, approaching the target from the southeast the massive Dominator was suddenly rocked by about twenty burst of heavy but inaccurate antiaircraft fire (flack) exploding at the correct

The Lady is Fresh the day it arrived at Floridablanca. Just the name was painted on the right side of the nose. (USAAF)

altitude but to their rear. Capt. Svore recalled that, "The antiaircraft fire was considerable but not real affective as being a single aircraft it was easy to vary altitude and direction than in a formation," to avoid the ground fire.

Arriving over the target at 1148 at an altitude of 15,000 ft the bombardier aligned the target in his sight and released all eight bombs that, when they reached the ground, exploded amongst a group of warehouse buildings in the southwest corner of the refinery. Prior to the mission the buildings were reported to be in good condition, but because of the flack received over the target post-strike photographs were not taken.

After *The Lady is Fresh* broke away from the target the two B-32's formed up in formation and headed home returning to Floridablanca at 1400 completing the 1,040 mile mission in six hours. The Dominators made it through their baptism of fire unscathed.

That same day SSgt Munsell was ordered to clean the forward top turret on his B-32. While going about his business cleaning the plexiglass dome inside the turret, "The hardstand our B-32 was parked on shook the plane rather hard. I thought I could hear someone talking and laughing inside the forward bomb bay. I got to the bomb bay and asked what was going on and I was told by the armorers who were ordered to change the bomb load, they were improvising on how quickly it could be done." The armorers had been ordered to change the bomb loads from twelve 1,000 lb bombs to forty 500 lb incendiary clusters. "They were defusing the bombs and dropping them from the bomb racks a little over fifteen feet to the hardstand below. Everything shook including me. I didn't stay to debate their logic and left the area immediately," he remembers.

16 June 1945

The following morning, after his encounter with the haphazard armorers, Jack Munsell was in a briefing with thirty-six other men, preparing for the mission that required the change in ordinance. This was the first mission that included all three of the super bombers. Each bomber had a crew of ten plus two trainees and an airplane commander for the mission. The crews discovered their bomb loads had been changed when they were assigned their target for the day, Tiato Town. For the second day in a row the B-32's would fly to the city, this time though the target was not just the refinery but the city itself.

At 0800 the Dominators began to leave Floridablanca. Jack Munsell was onboard one of the B-32's as the aerial flight engineer and recalled a conversation with the pilot. "After completing the preflight, the pilot told me what RPM he wanted on take off and then ordered me to give him twenty degree flaps at the tower during our take off run. I did. This was contrary to the G file (instruction manual) we studied, however the pilot was a major and I was a sergeant and things worked out very well."

The three Dominators flew in tight formation the 529 miles to Tiato with *Hobo Queen II* leading the formation, *The Lady is Fresh* was to its right and *528* off the left wing. As they reached the target area the crews dispensed "rope" to deflect the Japanese radar systems in response to the flack received by *The Lady is Fresh* on the previous mission. Rope was the American equivalent to the Royal Air Forces

All three B-32's on their hardstands at Floridablanca. The painting of the *Hobo Queen II* was not completed by the time of this photograph. (USAAF)

"Chaff," which were small squares of foil dropped around target areas in Europe that jammed German radar that was used to direct anti aircraft artillery. Instead of squares rope was strings of aluminum foil one inch wide and varying in length from 100 to 400 inches. At forty five miles out from Tiato each Dominator dispensed rope in five minute intervals. When they neared the target, this was increased to every two minutes.

As they reached Tiato, the formation was spread by 500 ft between each B-32 to ensure maximum coverage over the town. Just then, a burst of flack was received off the right side of the formation at the correct altitude but well off target. Jack Munsell noted that there were Japanese fighters in the air at the same altitude but just out of machine gun range; he felt they were more than likely directing the antiaircraft fire. In actuality, what he saw were North American P-51 Mustangs that were flying a separate mission to the island.

At 1030 they began their attack starting in the southeastern corner flying northwest over the town, at 19,000 ft the 500 lb incendiary bombs were released every 100 ft across the town to ensure that the entire town would be hit by at least one of the 120 bombs being dropped. The bombardiers achieved great success in the eyes of their crews which were enthusiastic by the results. All three crews observed that smoke and flames covered the center of town as they flew out of the target area.

During the post flight debriefing upon their return to Floridablanca the crews reported that high winds had spread the fires caused by the bombs to the northern portion of the town that hadn't been hit and the crews were excited about giving Tiato the "Tokyo Treatment." Two hours after the mission, bombers from the 43rd BG passed over Tiato and reported that the town was still burning.

In his journal Julie Kossor wrote about his second mission, "A little trouble on take off, damn cold in the ball. Made a beautiful bombing the whole town is burning, smoke up to 3000 ft. Seen four fighters; turned out to be P-51's. Got a few blast of Ack-Ack but no holes in the planes. B-24's went to hit the town. Said there was no town to hit. It was entirely burned out."

Also on 16 June, Col. Cook submitted to V Bomber Command a preliminary report on the effectiveness of the B-32 to date. Included in the report was the total flying hours of each aircraft, *Hobo Queen II* 112 hours, *The Lady is Fresh* 106 hours and *528* had flown just 85 hours due to plaguing maintenance issues. The majority of these hours were from the ferry flight and their use to train the new crews in correlation to the "B-32 School."

Along with the aircraft times were reports on the flight characteristics, positive performance notes, and information regarding the consumption of fuel and the use of auto pilot. The suitability of Floridablanca as a base of operations was summarized as, "No difficulties have been experienced in operating from the 7,000 ft airstrip and the hardstands" where the aircraft were parked. The B-32's taxied from the strip to hardstands where they were parked between missions and used the reverse pitch propellers to back in, facing the taxiways. The reverse pitch propellers were a "necessity for backing into the limited size hardstands and a definite requirement for group operations."

The final portion of the report focused on the crew reactions to the aircraft, and the completion of the test program. The pilots and co-pilots reported on the ease in which one learned to fly the B-32. The radar operators commentated that the use of radar was a necessity on the approach to a target because of the dense cloud cover usually experienced and, finally, the bombardiers were having no problems hitting their assigned targets. Col. Cook had no evidence that the completion date 1 July 1945 could not be achieved and to date three full crews had been trained and another three were to be ready by 23 June.

The first four missions had been completed under a strict vale of censorship that prohibited mentioning of the B-32 in press releases and in letters home. In a June entry Julie Kossor wrote, "Flying practice missions in B-32's, cannot write home about it, still a secret." Precautions were also taken by Col. Cook to ensure the safety of each bomber. Col. Cook had the final say in the air worthiness of each B-32 and as stated in the 312th BG's official history, "They were given the same attention that a mother shows a newborn child, however the targets were not milk runs."

One of the Cook Projects B-32's being refueled between missions. This could possibly be *Hobo Queen II* because a bomb bay fuel tank is lying on the ground under the bomber. (Authors collection)

On 17 June the Squadron received a message from Brig. Gen Crabb on the progress of the B-32 combat test to date.

"Congratulations upon your successful completion of the first four B-32 strikes in history, it is most commendable that these missions have been run without mishap or delay congruently with a big training program. The 312th continues to uphold its reputation for versatility."

17/18 June 1945

While *The Lady is Fresh* and *528* were conducting transition flights *Hobo Queen II* was readied for a new type of mission for the Dominator and its crews. The mission tested the B-32's ability to conduct searches by the use of radar and the ability to bomb a target relying solely on the use radar. The mission also tested the bombers effectiveness in attacking smaller targets such as ships, something the crews had not experienced by that time. The goal of the mission as stated in the 312th BG's official history says, "In ordered to disrupt Jap shipment of troops and supplies between Hainan Island and Indo China, one B-32 was assigned to conduct an armed recon of the Tonkin Gulf."

During the day on 17 June the maintenance crews set to work preparing *Hobo Queen II*. The main fuel tanks and two 1,500 gal tanks in the rear bomb bay were filled with 6,060 gal of aviation fuel for the twelve hour mission. In the forward bomb bay armorers had installed just nine 500 lb bombs for the night search mission. The crew of ten, plus three trainees and the airplane commander, were instructed prior to the mission that if shipping could not be found they were assigned a secondary target Hoihow Town on the northern tip of Hainan Island off China's eastern coast.

The crew of fourteen climbed aboard *Hobo Queen II* and left Floridablanca at 1900, flying over the South China Sea and arriving in the target area at approximately 2300. The pilot flew low over the sea

Hobo Queen II under guard at Floridablanca, two B-24's are behind it.
(Authors Collection)

at about 8,500 ft and conducted a radar and visual search. It was a rather dark evening and the costal towns were blacked out which hampered the visual search. However the crew did spot a row of six lights but determined them to be a pier. By 0200 a suitable shipping target hadn't been spotted and a decision was made by the airplane commander to call off the search and head for the secondary target.

Approaching the target from the southwest the crew dispensed rope on fifteen second intervals, starting fifteen miles out from the target even though there hadn't been any flack in route to the target. Reaching the target at 0248 at an altitude of just 8,500 ft over the town, the bombardier released all nine bombs that the crew witnessed bursting on the western portion of the town. Immediately after bombing their target the crew headed for home landing at 0745, completing the twelve hour mission safely.

19 June 1945

Ground crews worked thorough the night and into the early morning hours preparing all three B-32's. Twelve 1,000 lb bombs had been loaded into *The Lady is Fresh*. Both *Hobo Queen II* and *528* were loaded with just nine, 1,000 lb bombs, because bomb bay fuel tanks were installed in their rear bomb bays. The targets, as instructed by V Bomber Command, were two railroad bridges located at Paiyapai and Rokuryo, on the east coast of Formosa. The crews were also assigned a secondary target, a third bridge that was located near the town of Ikegami. The secondary target was only to be bombed if the crews experienced any trouble (i.e. weather) over the first two bridges.

The Lady is Fresh and *Hobo Queen II*, with crews of eleven onboard, left an hour prior to *528*, which was suffering from an electrical issue experienced during engine start up. Due to their late departure, the crew of *528* was ordered by Col. Cook to fly directly to the secondary target, the bridge at Ikegami. When the crew of *528* reached the east coast of Formosa they were greeted by the Japanese with two bursts of flack well below them at about 5,000 ft.

They continued towards the bridge from the northeast at an altitude of 9,500 ft and made their first drop on the bridge. Three of the bombs fell from *528* towards the bridge and the crew watched as their they exploded well to the west of the bridge. The pilot after regaining control of the bomber from the bombardier, who flew it while on the bomb run, made a wide turn to realign over the target. The crew pressed in for a second time from the northeast determined to make their mark on the bridge by dropping three more 1,000 pounders from 9,700 feet. Unfortunately, on this run the bombardier had overcorrected from the initial drop and the bombs fell into the river east of the bridge. There were only three bombs remaining in the belly of *528* as it approached the bridge for a third and final time, from the northeast.

The bombardier had the bridge in his site and flipped the release toggle, the Dominator lifted up slightly when the last three bombs were released. Anxiously watching the bridge the crew reported that two of the bombs appeared to be near hits. They were unable to determine the exact results though, since smoke from the previous explosions obstructed the view of the target. After the last run *528* turned for home.

The Lady is Fresh, the original nose art painted on *529.* (Noseartphotos.com)

Meanwhile the crews onboard *Hobo Queen II* and *The Lady is Fresh* flew in formation to the bridge at Paiyapai unnoticed by Japanese fighters or antiaircraft fire. The first pass over the bridge was made from the north by *Hobo Queen II* from an altitude of 10,000 ft, the bombardier lined the bridge up in his sight and released three 1,000 lb bombs over the target. The crew reported that one of the bombs exploded near the bridge. While *Hobo Queen II* was making its first run on the bridge, *The Lady is Fresh* was lining up behind it. From an altitude of 10,500 ft the bombardier dropped three bombs that exploded 500 ft northeast of the bridge. The crew aboard *The Lady is Fresh* then made a wide turn to make their second attack. On this pass only two bombs were dropped with a bit more accuracy as the bombs exploded in the river just fifty feet east of the bridge. The second run ended the attack on the bridge at Paiyapai and the Dominators turned their focus on the second bridge at Rokuryo.

Arriving first over the second bridge was *Hobo Queen II* from the northeast; the bombardier dropped three one thousand pounders from 10,000 ft that exploded near the bridge. *The Lady is Fresh* arrived soon after and dropped two bombs that fell just 100 ft away from the bridge. After a wide turn for a second pass and to give *The Lady is Fresh* a chance to bomb the target, *Hobo Queen II* arrived over the bridge to drop its last three bombs. The bombardier released his bombs but missed the bridge by 200 ft. *The Lady is Fresh* returned for its second attack. Three bombs were dropped, and the crew watched as the bombs exploded very near the bridge and then made their last turn to realign over the target from the northeast. Their last three bombs were dropped but failed to find their mark landing 200 ft east of the bridge.

After dispensing their payloads the crews of *Hobo Queen II* and *The Lady is Fresh* made one final pass to take photographs and turned for home, arriving back at Floridablanca at 1430 completing a six and one half hour mission.

20 June 1945

On the morning of 20 June all three Dominators were loaded with four 2,000 lb bombs and 5,000 gal of fuel in preparation for the next mission. The crews were informed by Col. Cook, during their preflight briefing, that the target was a Japanese railroad yard located near the port town of Suo on the island of Formosa. The crews of eleven per Dominator climbed aboard their bombers and began going through the preflight checks. When the crew of *Hobo Queen II* attempted to start their engines one of the four R-3350's was running rough, and Col. Cook decided to hold the bomber on the ground.

At 0700 *The Lady is Fresh* and *528* left Floridablanca and headed for Formosa. When the bombers reached 10,000 ft the gunners climbed into their turrets for the 700 mile flight. In route to the target the weather was observed by the crews as favorable until they reached the town of Karenko, where a heavy overcast obscured the ground under the Dominators as they continued on towards Suo. The cloud cover obstructed the view of the bombardiers who had been instructed to bomb the target visually. Their only course of action was to drop

528 parked on its hardstand at Floridablanca between missions. (Fredickson)

below the clouds a move that was extremely dangerous given the mountainous terrain around the target.

The hazards at Suo proved too much for the crew who opted for the assigned secondary target, the railway bridges north of Tiato that were hit on the previous day's mission. *The Lady is Fresh* arrived over the bridge at Paiyapai at 1115 from the northeast. From an altitude of 10,000 ft the bombardier lined up his target, but just as he got the bridge in sight and was about to release his bombs the view was obscured by a cloud causing the bombs to fall off course 3,000 ft southwest of the bridge.

By the time *528* was able to line up on the bridge it had become completely obstructed by cloud cover. Already at their assigned secondary target, the crew decided to head for a third. Tamari Town would be their new target. In the town were two large warehouses located on its west side. Approaching the town from the southeast *528* dropped down to just 4,300 ft and dropped all four 2,000 lb bombs. The bombs found their mark scoring direct hits on the two warehouses, sending plumes off thick black smoke into the air. As the Dominators left the target area the smoke was still rising and the crews headed for Floridablanca touching down at 1455 completing a nearly eight hour mission.

22 June 1945

The crews of *The Lady is Fresh* and *528* were briefed about their target as directed by V Bomber Command for 22 June. The target was a butonal refinery located near the town of Heito, Formosa. A second target, to be hit separately, consisted of a heavy gun emplacement nearby. *The Lady is Fresh* was loaded with seventy-eight 260 lb fragmentation bombs for attacking the gun emplacement and *528*, was loaded with forty 500 lb bombs for attacking the refinery. *Hobo Queen II* was grounded once again, this time due to an electrical issue with one of its engine's superchargers.

The Dominators, with crews eleven per bomber, left Florida-blanca led by *The Lady is Fresh* and flew in formation for Heito. Upon reaching the target, *The Lady is Fresh* moved in for the first attack from the northeast dispensing rope the entire length of the bomb run trying to combat the heavy but inaccurate antiaircraft fire that was violently jostling the bomber as it moved in for its attack. From 15,000 ft the bombardier dropped the seventy eight clusters on the gun position at 1052, missing it by 200 ft to the southeast. The bombs exploded amongst a group of barracks that housed the positions garrison, causing a considerable amount of damage.

528 made its attack on the butanol refinery at 1058 from an altitude of 15,000 ft, flying southwest through heavy flack that the crew reported was at altitude and on course. As they arrived over the target *528's* bombardier released thirty of the 500 lb bombs on the target below. The crew witnessed ninety percent of their bombs falling in the target areas with three large explosions amongst the buildings in the refinery which resulted in huge plumes of black smoke rising up to 5,000 ft. As *528* flew away from the target there were still ten bombs in the bomb bay that had hung up on the initial drop and were salvoed immediately after the crew left the target area.

The Dominators quickly made their exit from the target's vicinity to avoid any further flack. Both bombers made it through the barrage of flack undamaged and returned to Floridablanca six hours and forty minutes after their departure.

Members of the 312th BG looked over *Hobo Queen II* as the number two engine was being worked on. (USAAF via Hornbeck)

23/24 June 1945

By the following day the repairs to *Hobo Queen II* were finally completed, and it was readied for the second night radar mission of the combat test. Capt. Svore led the mission, with an additional ten crew members onboard. The B-32 was loaded with 6,000 gal of fuel, the extra bomb bay fuel tanks were installed in the rear bomb bay and a load of nine 500 lb bombs were loaded into the forward bomb bay. The crew left Floridablanca for the Macao Canton River on China's eastern coast. The entire mission was flown at less than 10,000 ft so the crew did not have to use oxygen on the lengthy mission, which was required on any flight above 10,000 ft.

Upon arrival in the search area, a single ship was sighted on the radar screen but was out of range. The crew continued to search through the darkness, but it soon proved fruitless and no other targets were identified. Capt. Svore then decided to call off the search and they headed for the secondary target, an airstrip located on the eastern coast of China. Col. Svore remembered seeing the lights of Hong Kong as they flew inland and recalled, "This was a mission that relied solely on radar, could have been a surprise to the Japanese that the Americans could cover so far into China."

Seven miles out from the target rope was dispensed to deter any possible resistance to their attack. Capt. Svore and his crew arrived over the Sanchau aerodrome at 0157, at an altitude of just 1,000 ft. This bomb run was different than any other B-32 bomb run made during the war because it was conducted solely by radar and not visually because of a moderate cloud cover over the target. The bombs were dropped, but only six of the nine fell to the target, the other three had hung up in the bomb bay. The crew reported seeing only one explosion through the overcast 100 ft west of the airstrip. After the bombs were released, Capt. Svore ordered the crew to continue dispensing rope for the next seven miles as *Hobo Queen II* flew away from the target, but the Japanese never opposed the attack.

The three bombs that hung up were salvoed into the ocean off Sanchau Island. On the return trip, a green light was spotted twenty miles off the right wing and was watched for an hour and a half before disappearing into the night. The crew returned to Floridablanca, completing the eleven hour mission without any opposition.

25 June 1945

On the morning of 25 June the same two Dominators that began the combat test conducted the tenth and final mission. The crews of eleven were gathered for the mission briefing and given their target, railroad bridges north of Hatto railway station at Kiirun, a town 744 miles from Floridablanca, on the north end of Formosa. The target was a major link in the Japanese supply system. During the briefing the crews were warned about the possibility of heavy flack and aggressive Japanese fighter opposition. Even with this warning there was not a fighter escort assigned. Earlier that morning the armorers had loaded *The Lady is Fresh* with twelve 1,000 lb bombs and *Hobo Queen II* with just nine 1,000 lb bombs because the bomb bay fuel tanks were still installed in the rear bomb bay from the previous night's mission. *528*, was left behind just as it had been on the first missions, because of a maintenance issue. A hole had burnt through the nose ring cowl on the number two engine and a replacement part was not readily available.

They left Floridablanca and over a light cloud cover headed for their target. At 10,000 ft the gunners climbed into their turrets and kept a close eye to the sky looking for any sign of Japanese fighters as they approached the target. The 744 mile flight to the target lasted three and a half hours according to the official unit history, which was three minutes behind schedule. *Hobo Queen II* was the first bomber over the target. The crew released rope on the approach but there was no opposition in route to or over the target. From an altitude of 20,000 ft the Bombardier looked down at the target below through his Norden bombsight and found the bridge blanketed by a thick layer of clouds. When suddenly a hole appeared in the cloud cover and he quickly released his nine 1,000 lb bombs on the target below, which exploded 1,000 ft northeast of the bridge.

Next in was *The Lady is Fresh*. As the bombardier looked through his bombsight, all he could see was the thick layer of clouds that obscured the target. After an initial pass the airplane commander decided that the cloud cover was too thick and opted for a target of opportunity, the town of Giren. Approaching the target from the north *The Lady is Fresh* rumbled over the town at an altitude of 20,000 ft. The bombardier aligned his sight on the center of Giren and released his twelve bombs, which the crew watched exploding directly on target. Upon completion of the mission, the crew reported that the bombs had damaged several of the buildings within the target area.

When *The Lady is Fresh* completed its bomb run they headed for home in formation. The crews were relieved that there was no opposition during the entire flight and settled in for the fight home returning to Floridablanca seven and a half hours after their departure, ending the B-32 combat test.

The combat test had concluded, without a major incident, loss of a B-32 due to enemy fire, or an accident during the regular training flights. The gunners had sat by their guns on each mission but the Japanese fighters never came up to contest even one of their missions, much to the crew's delight.

An unidentified B-32 being "checked over" by curious G.I.'s, a sight that was repeated at each stop throughout the war. (Authors Collection)

CHAPTER 7

THE COOK REPORT

The mission on 25 June 1945 marked the completion of the combat test. As soon as the mission concluded Col. Cook began to compile all of the data gathered which was required for his report. During the test program eleven combat missions had been flown between 29 May 1945 and 25 June 1945. The test program concluded six days ahead of its scheduled completion date of 1 July 1945. Throughout the "Cook Project" the three B-32's had accumulated a combined total fly time of 572 hours and forty-five minutes during combat missions and training flights. *The Lady is Fresh* had flown the most, a total of 218 hours and ten minutes followed by *Hobo Queen II,* with 190 hours and ten minutes, and *528* had only flown 164 hours and twenty five minutes; mainly due to the mechanical issues suffered throughout the test period.

Twenty-three days after the last mission of the combat test Col. Cook submitted his final report to the Commanding General of V Bomber Command. In his report, Col. Cook outlined the progress of the "B-32 School," made a list of critical and recommended changes to be made to the bomber and gave overall crew reactions to the B-32 prior to his overall approval of the Dominator.

The first portion of the report focused on the issues crews encountered throughout the test which were in need of immediate attention. This included the availability of spare parts such as engines and nacelle's which cover the engines. Col. Cook had been informed of their availability from Valtee, Consolidated's sister company, but this still plagued the B-32's in the combat zone. Consolidated and the USAAF's claims about the "priority" and the abundance of spare parts was ultimately false, and led to the numerous groundings throughout the B-32's short combat career.

The B-32's had a weight restriction of 110,000 lbs placed on them by the ATSC during the early tests on the B-32 and by the time they went to war the restrictions were still in place because static load tests had not been completed. Col. Cook, in his report, called for the lifting of this restriction because the required test had been completed and the B-32 met the necessary requirements. Col. Cook reinforced his statement by stating in his report, "It can be pointed out that no basic structural deficiencies have been noted to date."

The final items covered in the first part of the report are minor notes asking for radio countermeasure equipment to be flown over on the anticipated next batch of B-32's to be installed on *528*, since it had been completed just prior to its attachment to the "Cook Project" this equipment was left off. Col. Cook also suggested a change in the camera used to enable the crew to take larger photographs than that of the previously installed camera.

The second portion of the report gave a summary of the crew transitioning. By the time the report was submitted to V Bomber Command there were a total of twelve combat crews nearing the completion of their training which began just fifteen days earlier. Col. Cook outlined that further training would be required in the use of radar navigation, and more importantly radar trained bombardiers. He asked for more aircraft to complete this objective in a timely fashion, along with the training of flight crews on instrument only landings. He continued saying "Personnel in the theater learn rapidly. This is influenced by the fact that the man will not be required to postpone the use of the skill he picks up". This was due to the training being so interactive and the fact that it was completed in the most efficient manner. The final thing that Col Cook referred to; in terms of the crew training, was a request for more aircraft, "A considerable portion of the group effort which could be used for combat effort if trained personnel were assigned (and the) early deliveries of more aircraft."

The majority of the 206 hours and five minutes of flying time the B-32's accumulated during just the month of June were spent on training missions. Due to this, Col. Cook requested aircraft to be sent to the combat zone to be used exclusively for use in training. He stressed that for normal combat operations to take place more aircraft should be sent as soon as possible because more training was needed than could be offered in the field. He felt if the training continued on a mission-to-mission basis the effectiveness of the unit would severely decline.

Attached to the report was an annex that thoroughly covered the bomber. It began with a list of three "Critical items" as referred to as by Col. Cook. The list was relatively short and in Col. Cook's words, "A long list including many difficult critical items is not required." The first item mentioned were a lack of wing deicing units and the need for additional heating of the crew compartments. Jack Munsell complained about the fact that crews in the pacific weren't issued the same cold weather gear, such as electrically heated flying suits, as bomber crews in the European Theater. Col. Cook recommended that Consolidated engineers should be, "dispatched to this theater, bringing all the data on the latest changes and parts for field installations".

The second issue focused around the Sperry nose and tail turrets. "The nose and tail turrets are considered the most important turrets in this theater," explained Col. Cook. Japanese fighter pilots had a tendency to attack from the rear or head on as the B-32 crews would find out in the months to come. The turrets had a couple of drawbacks though, the ammunition feed belts were being pinched between the walls of the fuselage and the turret when rotated causing it to jamb, as was the case on 29 May 1945. Col. Cook recommended that the ammunition feeding issues be resolved as soon as possible. Secondly, the clutch that operated the turrets were overheating and burning out, which was due to the turret being operated when the clutch was only partially engaged. Col. Cook recommended new clutches being installed that would not allow the turret to be operated without the clutch being fully engaged.

The main landing gear strut, each wheel was fifty six inches in diameter. Note the open bomb bay doors behind the GI who is more than likely not a naval mechanic but an USAAF mechanic who found a hat he liked. Also the Navy was never assigned a B-32. (Authors Collection)

The final "Critical item" focused around the troublesome R-3350 engines. The exhaust collectors for the engines were too weak and needed to be made of stronger material, the clamps holding the collectors together were failing and bending. This caused the exhaust to escape and burn out sections of the engine. The nuts that attached the collectors to the engines were backing off, thus allowing the collectors to come lose during operation. Col. Cook requested replacement parts for all three of these issues and made another request that fifty percent of the parts manufactured be for use as spares, yet another example of the lack of availability of spare parts.

The remaining portion of the report is a complete overview of the aircraft, and a list of "Clean up items" as referred to by Col. Cook. Included in this portion were crew reactions about their stations and the handling of the aircraft. The navigators gave the most glowing of all responses, "The B-32 is an airplane built around navigators table. It is the best arrangement that could be imagined", the report stated. The bombardiers reported that even with limited viewing from the position around the bombsite there were no problems hitting the targets due to visibility. The communication officers submitted the final portion stating, "The location and operation of the radio installations is considered very good and is well suited to the B-32." The layout of the flight deck was reported to aid in communication between the flight crew. The feedback reflected the majority of the crew's overall positive feelings about the B-32.

There was one group to complain, the bombardiers negatively commented on the lack of a vision on either side of the Norden bomb sight. Col. Cook described their issue as the, "Ungentlemanly attitudes which have to be assumed at times when searching around the site," for the target. Even with the bombardier's discomforts Col. Cook reported the issues had not affected the bombardier's abilities to drop the bombs on target.

The maintaining of the B-32's was a hot and cold issue. Col. Cook wrote, "The required maintenance on the airplanes was much less than expected. This has contributed much to the success of the project." The majority of the problems encountered by the maintenance crews were due to the lack of available spare parts. The issue was addressed by Col. Cook requesting that further shipments should be sent with the next batch of Dominators, or ahead of them, if possible.

He pointed out that the only spare parts that had been received were those that arrived with the B-32's on their ferry flight from the United States. The other issue faced by the maintenance crews was the lack of permanent facilities. The ground crews were forced to use portable equipment and equipment that was not produced with the B-32 in mind. Col. Cook recommended that a permanent facility be chosen so maintenance facilities could be constructed.

Col. Cook described the flight characteristics as "Very favorable;" formation flying was excellent due to the handling of the aircraft, although because there were just three B-32's in the test program the information was deemed as incomplete. During the transition flights landings had posed only a couple of minor issues consisting of two tailskids being damaged. Also, during the training flights, Col. Cook noted that the distance required for takeoff varied between 3,000 to 5,000 feet depending on the wind and the experience of the pilot.

The final portion of the report was on the overall suitability of the B-32 as an effective weapon. Col. Cook stated that, "Combat test crews and the eleven crews now being checked off are having no difficulty with handling of the airplane, due to the ease of transitioning it has been possible to check crews off more rapidly." The offensive capabilities showed "Excellent results." The types of bombing included both visual and radar assisted from various altitudes, the highest at 20,000 feet. Many of the runs were aided by radar due to the common occurrence of cloud cover in route to the target.

The combat suitability portion concluded with a review of the defensive armament, which could not be realistically gauged because of the lack fighter opposition. Aside from the jamming problems experienced in the nose and tail turrets, the defensive armament was considered to be "adequate." The report overall, shed positive light on the B-32 as an effective weapon and offered insight to the role it could have played in the Pacific as a powerful companion to the B-29.

A head on view of *The Lady is Fresh* at Clark Field. (USAAF via Hornbeck)

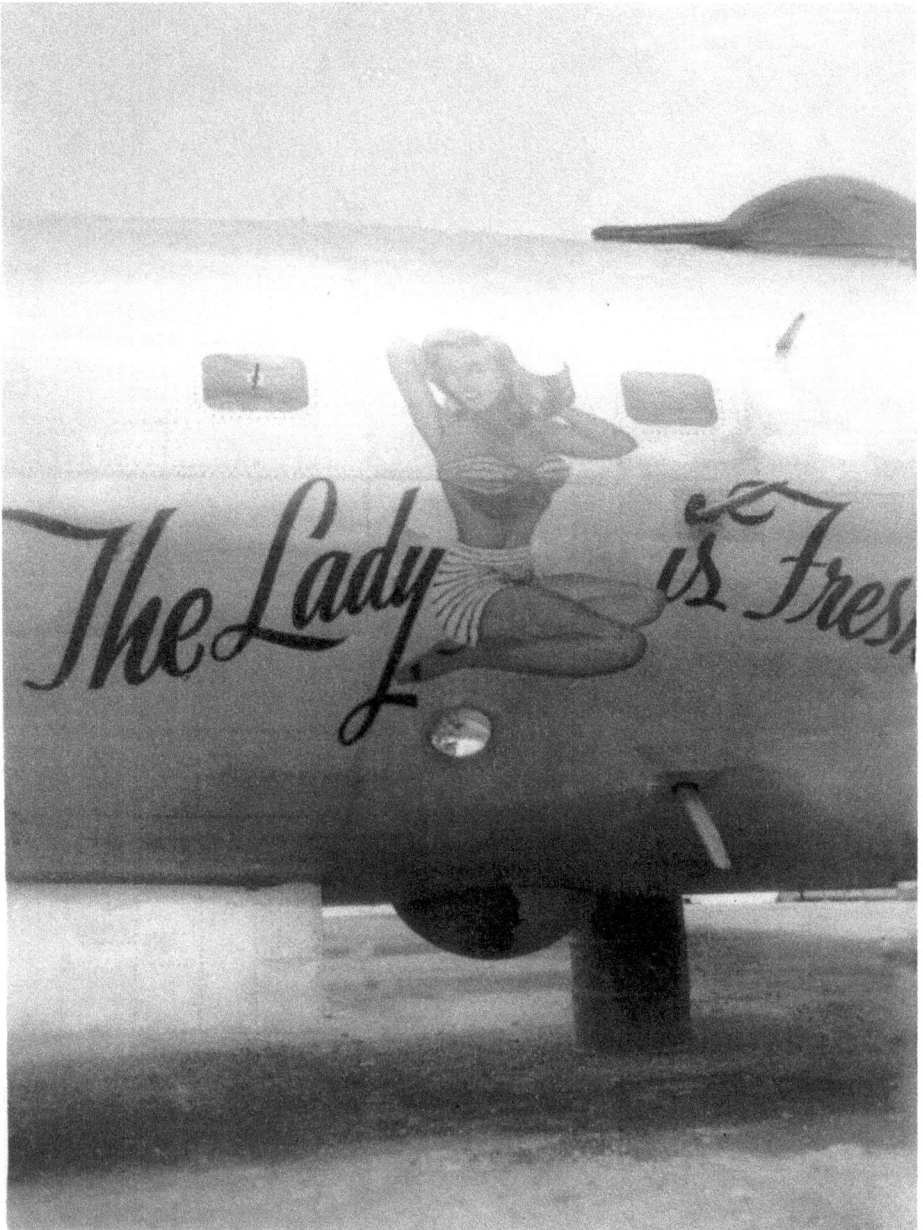

The new nose art added to *The Lady is Fresh* prior to the end of the war, which was re-painted on the left side of the fuselage replacing the previous art work. (Authors Collection)

The replacement nose art of *Hobo Queen II,* it was moved from under the cockpit window to the left side of the fuselage, pictured prior to its accident. (Authors Collection)

CHAPTER 8

386th BS VERY HEAVY

July was a relatively quiet month for the 386th BS; in the terms of combat missions flown, but the planes and transition crews were kept very busy. The B-32 school continued a grueling schedule of training flight crews throughout the month. Officially during July the 386th BS Light was re-designated Very Heavy as it officially became the first B-32 squadron.

In early July the men of the 387th BS were transferred to the 388th and 389th BS's that were still flying A-20 Havocs, as the 387th BS was re-designated as a B-32 squadron. However though, the 387th BS never was assigned a B-32. Some members of the 386th and 387th were temporarily assigned to the 22nd and 43rd BG's that were flying B-24 Liberators to be familiarized with the use of heavy four engine bombers due to lack of B-32's made available to meet the demands of training. Upon completion of their training, the crews returned to Floridablanca to complete their transition onboard the three B-32's which rarely got a break during their combat careers.

6 July 1945

Only two combat missions were flown in the month of July. On the morning of 6 July 1945 *Hobo Queen II, The Lady is Fresh,* and *528* were each loaded with twelve 1,000 lb bombs. The target was a sugar refinery being used to make butonal located at Teko Town, Formosa. According to the 312th BG's official history, the crews were accompanied by a guest bombardier from Headquarters.

Once the bombers reached the Formosa coast line there was a medium cloud cover, so the crews decided to use radar to guide them to the target. The Dominators reached their target at 1104 and they were immediately greeted by the Japanese with heavy anti aircraft fire. The flack was mostly inaccurate but in one case the fiberglass retractable radar dome on an unidentified B-32 was damaged. Over the target the guest bombardier had little success, the crews observed only six of the bombs falling on the target causing minimal damage. Upon arrival back at Luzon the guest bombardier blamed his inaccuracy on the cloud cover over the target. The official narrative of the mission sates, "No damage was done, nothing was accomplished."

13 July 1945

The mission for the night of 13 July was scheduled as a single aircraft, low level shipping search. *The Lady is Fresh* left Floridablanca and headed out over the North China Sea. Not long into the flight, the crew encountered rough weather and was forced to return home. Due to the weather and shortened duration of the flight the crew was unable to spot any shipping and returned home with a full bomb load.

Five days later, on 18 July, Julie Kossor flew a transition flight that lasted three hours and fifty minutes. The training flight was a low altitude lesson on attacking shipping. Just twenty feet off the water they dropped their bombs. Four days later he flew another transition flight on 22 July and wrote, "Another transition flight got caught in a storm." To make matters worse the navigator got disoriented in the storm and struggled to find the way back to Floridablanca. "Finally made it home and landed in a rainstorm, rough landing" he wrote in his final entry about transition training.

By the end of July the constant training flights were beginning to take their toll on the civilian instructors and the B-32's. By the end of June the lack of available spare parts was becoming a serious issue with each flight. On average, it took a B-32 nine man-hours to be prepared for a mission; but with the lack of replacement engines and exhaust stacks, maintenance crews were forced to become creative with their repairs and as the training flights continued the wear and tear on the engines and landing gear slowly took their toll. The work was still hampered by the lack of permanent maintenance facilities, the fact that parts often had to be improvised in the field, and the portable equipment not always suited for the B-32.

As the monotonous crew training progressed some the B-24 crews who had been transferred into the transition program felt they had been "Sandbagged" and began to openly gripe, as many had acquired enough points for rotation and began to boycott the training classes conducted by the civilian factory representatives. At the same time, the company representatives were grumbling about the lack of sufficient training the B-24 pilots were receiving before moving on to becoming instructor pilots with very little classroom instruction, and even less flying experience. Unfortunately, when the civilians voiced their opinions to the military commanders they were abruptly talked down.

On 29 July the B-32 was formally introduced to select members of the press who were in the Philippines. Col. Cook took them up for an introductory flight in *Hobo Queen II*. One of the correspondents was James E Hutchenson, of the Associated Press. During the flight Col. Cook remarked to them, "The B-32 takes off like a fighter, faster than smaller bombers." Once at altitude Col. Cook offered the correspondents a turn at the controls, under close supervision of his co-pilot Lt. H.W. Rehm Jr. When Hutchenson took his turn he remarked that, "It responded surprisingly easily to an amateurs touch." Col. Cook further explained that, "B-32 strikes had been exceedingly accurate against bridges, airfields and industrial plants." In regards to transition training he told them, "Liberator crews can be trained to operate the new plane successfully in a week's ground school and a week's flight training."

On 31 July 1945, 5th AF command officially ordered the 386th and 387th BS's to transfer to Yontan airfield, on the recently captured island of Okinawa. This brought the B-32's closer to Japan, for their use in pre-invasion strikes on the Japanese home islands. Starting on 1 August personnel of the 386th BS began moving to Okinawa. The maintenance crews, officers and *528* arrived on the 8 August.

The previous evening the crew of *528*, including Julie Kossor, were ordered to Okinawa on 7 August. The bomber was loaded with fuel and bombs, because they were ordered to patrol, on their way to Okinawa, for enemy shipping. By dawn though, no ships were spotted and they headed for Okinawa. They arrived early in the morning of 8 August 1945 with their bomb load still in the bomb bay which was a hair-raising experience. Upon their arrival, Julie Kossor noted that, "Yontan harbor was filled with about 300 ships and the airstrip has about 500 different planes on it." The move was completed on 11 August when *Hobo Queen II* arrived. *The Lady is Fresh* remained at Floridablanca awaiting a replacement engine and didn't arrive at Okinawa until 20 August.

Searchlights above Yontan on one of the many nights the Japanese paid a visit.
(Authors Collection)

Their new home proved to be an ideal fit, "Because of the 1,250 mile range, 20,000 pound bomb load, Davis wing and reverse pitch propellers it was an ideal plane for Okinawa," stated Gen. Ennis White Head, the newly appointed commander of the 5th AF at the end of the war. When at Yontan the crews were kept busy. During the day transition training picked up right where it had left off at Floridablanca and at night the Japanese reminded them that the war was not yet quite over, "Had an aircraft alert every night were here. One night thirty four Japanese fighters strafed us, thirty two shot down by anti aircraft and our fighters," recalled Julie Kossor.

On 12 August the 386th BS received four additional B-32's serial numbers *42-108530,* which had been originally scheduled for the "Cook Project", *42-108539, 42-108543 and 42-108544.* A fifth Dominator, *42-108578* arrived the fallowing day on 13 August bringing the total number of B-32's in the Pacific to eight. By the end of the month the ninth and final B-32, *42-108531,* joined the squadron but never participated on any of the remaining few combat missions.

The old meets new, in the foreground are Consolidated B-24's and to the far left are two B-32's which had just arrived at Yontan. In the background are hundreds of aircraft including B-24's, B-25's, C-46's, C-47's, P-38's and four more B-32's. (Authors Collection)

13/14 August 1945

In August, five offensive combat missions were flown, mainly comprised of night radar search missions for Japanese shipping. The first of these was during the evening of 13 August. Two B-32's loaded with nine 500 lb bombs, and bomb bay fuel tanks, left Okinawa at 2130. They headed for the Korean coast to patrol the waters of the Tsu-Shima Strait. The bombers split up. One patrolled the Korean coast but spotted no activity. The other Dominator located a ship and made a run dropping all nine bombs, scoring two near misses that damaged the, ship causing it to list. A second ship was spotted some time later but because they had dropped all of their bombs on the previous ship, the crew could only fire their machine guns as they passed over. The two Dominators returned to Yontan without facing any opposition and were unscathed.

42-108578 after its arrival on 3 August 1945, days later it took part in the last aerial combat of World War II. (USAAF)

That evening *528* left Yontan at 2320 for a patrol along the coasts of two of the Japanese islands Kyushu and Honshu. A visual and radar guided search was conducted and one ship was spotted on the radar screen. The pilot of *528* turned the massive bomber in the ships direct and made his attack. The bombardier, once over the ship released his bombs, scoring direct hits, and the ship quickly sank. Upon their arrival at Okinawa, the number one engine was on fire. As soon as *528* came to a stop the ground crews were able to extinguish the fire while the crew escaped unharmed. Unfortunately, the engine was a total loss and minor damage was inflicted on the wing taking the bomber out of action until replacement parts were available.

14/15 August 1945

For the second evening in as many nights the Tsu-Shima Strait was searched for shipping. Three B-32's left Okinawa at 1840 and flew to the strait, conducting a low level radar and visual search that lasted until dawn. The crews were unsuccessful in locating any targets and all three Dominators returned to Okinawa on the morning of 15 August.

15 August 1945

This mission marked the final offensive combat mission for the B-32. Two Dominators left Yontan heading in the direction of Honshu and the southern coast of Korea to conduct a search for Japanese air activity in the area. As the Dominators reached the search area they were radioed by the communications staff back on Okinawa to turn back. The Japanese had finally accepted the surrender terms offered by the Allies.

16 August 1945

Starting on 16 August the B-32 Dominator began a new role as aerial photographers. The new mission was to photograph Japanese airfields to determine their use for landing occupations forces, administration officials, and evacuating prisoners of war. The mission on 16 August started at 0530 when *Hobo Queen II* and *543* left Okinawa to photograph the Tokyo area. Immediately after the crews finished photographing the airfields they headed for home. As they reached the southern coast of Japan one of *543*'s engines suddenly caught fire. The crew attempted to extinguish the flames but was unsuccessful and the fire continued to burn the entire way back to Okinawa. Over Tokyo the Dominators met no opposition, but the situation changed drastically in the following days.

17 August 1945

Two days after the official cease-fire was agreed on the 386th BS was assigned to continue photographing airfields in the Tokyo area on the morning of 17 August. The mission would not have been

42-108539 and another Dominator prior to the mission of 17 August, after their arrival from the States, on 17 August *539* was heavily damaged during a battle over Tokyo and was written off. (Authors Collection)

112

necessary if Japanese officials would have complied with a request by Gen. Macarthur for detailed reports on the condition of airfields in the Tokyo area, but nothing was submitted. So four B-32's were assigned to the mission, *Hobo Queen II, 539, 543,* and *578* left Yontan at 0530. The crews were unprepared for the events that would occur hours later, summed up by Julie Kossor as, "The roughest mission I ever had."

The Dominators arrived over Tokyo at 1015. Each aircraft had been assigned separate targets and upon their arrival they broke formation, flying two miles apart, allowing each aircraft to photograph their objective. The commander of the 312th BG, Lt. Col. Selmon Wells piloted *543* and made the first run of the morning. Due to a dense overcast above the primary airfields the other B-32's were forced to photograph secondary targets including Imab and Yokosuka airfields.

At noon as Lt. Col. Wells broke off his photo run, a Japanese Tojo fighter pulled up alongside at 20,000 feet. The Tojo suddenly broke away and turned back towards *543* from two o'clock and opened fire. In response Lt. Col. Wells turned his massive bomber into the

42-108543 being refueled between missions, the Dominator required nearly 8,000 gallons of aviation fuel. (USAAF)

fighter's path allowing the nose and forward top turret gunners a better line of fire. The return fire spooked the fighter pilot enough for him to quickly break off his attack, and the crew of *543* became the first B-32 attacked by an enemy aircraft in the bombers brief history. It was only a brief moment in the mission but the situation soon turned drastic.

Reports about the antiaircraft fire varied by crew, the official battle report stated that the flack, "Was heavy but inaccurate" over Imba and Yokosuka. Julie Kossor and the crew of *543*, which viewed things quite differently, "The antiaircraft fire was heavy and damn accurate, just off our wing." Over Yokosuka they were hit in the left wing and the number four engine. In attempts to combat the flack, rope was dropped and the flack soon fell off.

Unfortunately, the flack never subsided, even when the Japanese own aircraft were in the vicinity. Ten fighters jumped the formation making single, uneager passes. "My ball (turret) wasn't down. Lt. Col. Wells, our pilot said it made the ship drag. I had to work on (retracting) the ball while the fighters attacked us," wrote Julie Kossor after the battle. Noticing the damage inflicted on *543* the Japanese swarmed and began to attack. "They attacked us from each wing and passed under my ball. A perfect target, but because I obeyed orders we may have crashed in Tokyo," he continued. During the attack a box had fallen on the radar operator and the crew thought he had been hit.

The first attack was head on, a Tojo aimed straight for the cockpit. The nose turret gunner opened fire and claimed to have witnessed his tracers hitting the fighter. After the battle, the crew scored it as damaged. The next pass was from two o'clock, made on the top turrets. One of the gunners, Sgt. Bert Woolkind watched as his rounds hit the fighter, "I gave him three bursts," causing its engine to emit black smoke and the fighter quickly pulled away and passed under *543*. Sgt. Woolkind claimed a probable kill. As the battle unfolded Julie Kossor noted that, "Lt. Col Wells yelled like a five year old kid when the planes attacked us."

While *543* was fighting off attacks, *539* piloted by Sec. Lt. S. Frick, was experiencing engine trouble that separated them from the formation, usually a death sentence for any bomber. Luckily for the crew, the Japanese were reluctant in their attacks, but a high number of hits were scored causing significant damage including a large hole in the left wing.

The Japanese again turned their attention to *543* when its tail turret jammed. The fighters continued their assault but from a distance making quick hit and run attacks on *543,* tearing holes in the rudder and the left wing. Then, just as soon as the attack had begun it was over.

The Japanese switched their focus to *578*, with Col. Svore at the controls, "They made at least twelve passes at us. They kept coming from all directions." A total of five Tojo's and one Tony moved in. The first attack made by the Tony came from underneath, as the fighter climbed up and over the Dominator. As the Tony passed the rear top turret gunner he squeezed off a burst from the twin .50 caliber machine guns and hit it, causing it to smoke and burst into flames as it suddenly rolled over and began to dive towards the ground. With those shots *578* scored the first official B-32 kill.

After watching the Tony go down, the remaining Japanese pilots became even more timid. The next attacker passed under the bomber and the ball turret gunner was able to squeeze off a few bursts, but the Tojo escaped unharmed. *578*'s tail turret was jamming and the Japanese were still attacking. The last three passes were made on the tail as Col. Svore decided to make a run for the sea, putting distance between him and the pursuers, marking the end of the battle.

The crew of *Hobo Queen II* escaped the mission unharmed. On the return flight back to Okinawa the crew of *543* ate lunch. Julie Kossor recalls, "On the way back everyone got sick. The sandwiches we had for lunch were poisoned by aluminum. Lt. Col. Wells, the pilot, navigator, bombardier and all the gunners got sick including myself." Five of the crewmembers remained in the hospital for a few days after the flight to recover.

Upon their arrival at Yontan fifty-nine hits were counted on *539*. The landing gear had been severely damaged, the left wing tip had a gapping hole in it, also the rudder and engine nacelle had been damaged by the flack and fighters. Due to the damage it was decided to use *539* for spare parts. The damage to *543* was repaired during the night and readied for the mission which was scheduled the next day.

The mission lasted roughly eleven hours and twenty-five minutes, with the combat consisting of twenty long minutes. The gunners collectively claimed one Tojo shot down, one Tony as a probable and another Tojo as damaged.

The gunners, wishing they had paid closer attention to Robert Nova during their training classes on the A-17 nose and tail turrets, went to him in the middle of the night of 17 and 18 August. "I remember being woken up by the gunners who wanted to know how to bore sight the turrets (aligning the barrels of a gun with the sight)." They had little success earlier that day shooting down the attacking aircraft and wanted to improve the accuracy of their turrets. "So we worked through the rest of the night. It was clear we used the stars (as targets). It worked great."

Also that evening a writer from the United Press interviewed the survivors of the mission and those working throughout the night repairing the B-32's. One of those men was ground crewman Sgt. Nunzio Locastro, "I thought the war was over, but look for yourself," he said, as he patched holes in 539's left wing tip, engine nacelles and rudder. Sgt. Bert Woolkind who claimed a probable kill remarked, "It's still a rough war." Finally, top turret gunner Sgt. Joseph Waller weighed in, "I don't feel much like the war is over. If this is the Japs' (sic) idea of peace, then I have a few ideas about peace for them."

News of the attack hit home on the morning of 18 August, causing widespread outrage, one of those angered was Sen. Dennis Chavez of New Mexico. Who was quoted in the 18 August edition of the New York Times, "It must not happen again. Any attacks on our planes, that surely were over there for observation purposes only, indicates war like attitude, at least by the officers involved. Let us hope that the Japanese authorities, whoever they may be at the moment understand it must not happen again." If anyone in the Japanese Empire understood the cease-fire terms it should have been those in Tokyo.

It was reported that on 18 August General Macarthur had told the Japanese that bombing missions had been halted but, unfortunately, he never mentioned the photographic missions being conducted by bombers. Col. Svore felt that the Japanese must have been very worried about the smaller numbers of bombers flying over, since the atomic bombing missions were flown by small groups of B-29's. For the battered B-32's and their crews 18 August would prove even more challenging.

18 August 1945

Morning came quickly for the crewmen who had worked through the night bore sighting their turrets. At the morning briefing the crews learned they would return to Tokyo for a third day in a row. They were also warned to expect opposition again; and they were not disappointed, as the "Peculiar peace," persisted.

Hobo Queen II, 543, 544 and *578* left Okinawa 0700 for the flight to Tokyo. Capt. Svore was onboard *578* as the flight and aircraft commander. *543* had been repaired over night and *544* replaced *539* which was out of service. In route to the target, *543* and *544* both suffe-

544 at Yontan , note the B-24's parked behind it. It was anticipated that all of the B-24 units in the Pacific would be replaced by B-32's. (Authors Collection)

red oil leaks and were forced to turn back for Okinawa, leaving *Hobo Queen II* and *578* to continue the mission.

The Dominators photographed Shimoshizo, Kicroshi and Imba airfields that were obscured the previous day and began their return flight back to Okinawa, when the trouble started. To the rear antiaircraft fire began to explode at their altitude but about 1,000 feet away. The flack was brief and caused minor damage to *578*. The Dominators quickly used electronic countermeasures to jamb the radar. In response the Japanese scrambled their fighters, fourteen Zeke's, Tony's and Tojo's attacked from the south.

Hobo Queen II flown by Capt. J. Klein and co-pilot Lt. Glen W. Bowie was their first intended victim. At 0125 three quick passes were made on the rear top turret from about eleven o'clock. All three quickly broke off their attacks as soon as the gunner returned fire. As the first three disappeared a Tojo moved in from three o'clock but it broke away when the ball turret gunner fired at it. A second Tojo made a pass on the tail, but it too broke off when fired at. The last attacks were made on the nose. The first fighter came in from one o'clock. The nose turret gunner got the attacker in his sights and opened up with his two .50 caliber machine guns. The rounds tore into the fighter; it rolled to its right leaving a trail of smoke behind it. *Hobo Queen II* had drawn first blood scoring a probable kill. After watching the fighter go down the other Japanese broke off leaving *Hobo Queen II* unscathed after just nine passes. Unfortunately the same could not be said for *578*.

While *Hobo Queen II* was being assaulted the crew of *578* was fighting for its survival. "By actual count of the camera men and gunners we had seventeen fighters on us," said Col. Svore. The attacks had been the same as the previous day, vigorous single ship passes. The first attacks by the Japanese were made on the tail where Sgt. John T. Houston was manning the Sperry A-17 tail turret. As the fighters came into range of his guns he opened fire and the pursuers immediately fell back out of range. Unfortunately, not all of the attackers were so timid.

Col. Svore remembered, "We were hopelessly out gunned as the Zero's were very aggressive." During one pass hits were made on the number three engine and a trail of smoke from the engine signaled to the Japanese to attack. Capt. Svore ordered the pilot Lt. John R. Anderson and his co-pilot Lt. R.E. Thomas, to feather the prop and Lt. Anderson radioed Capt. Klein onboard *Hobo Queen II* asking him, "If they could slow down, my number three is shot out and I can't keep up with you." Before Capt. Klein could respond, a Japanese pilot remarked in English over the intercom, "Yes please slow down so I can catch you and shoot you down." When asked by an Associated Press reporter after the mission, about his response, Lt. Anderson stated that his reply was un-printable but continued on saying, "If that Jap *(sic)* understands English as well as he speaks it, his ears are still red hot."

With the conclusion of the brief conversation the Japanese began to swarm the stricken bomber. The nose turret suddenly jammed and could not rotate from side to side. In the heat of the action an issue that had plagued the B-32 from its first combat mission reared its ugly head for second time as the fighters were lining up to spray the nose with cannon fire.

578 days after the attacks of 17 and 18 August 1945. Note the three Japanese flags painted under the cockpit window symbolizing the three fighters its crew shot down during the two days of engagements over Tokyo. (Author Collection)

The nose turret gunner, seeing this, began trying to escape the turret before it was hit, when he realized the fighter was at the same level that the turret was jammed. He quickly crawled back in and hit the dead man switch firing both .50 caliber M2 machine guns and unleashed on his victim. The rounds slammed into the fighter, causing it to smoke and descend and a highly unlikely probable kill was scored. Just after the drama in the nose, a zero attacked the tail. Sgt. Anderson hadn't noticed it until it had closed to about 1,200 yards away. At 1,000 yards he opened fire and upon his third burst the zero exploded into a ball of fire, the first kill of the day.

The excitement was short lived. Another fighter closed in from three o'clock and peppered the rear crew compartment. SSgt. Lacharite and Sgt. Anthony Marchione, photographers, were busy at work, snapping pictures throughout the attack. When the rounds tore into the aft section of the Dominator both men were wounded in the legs. Just as SSgt. Lacharite began administering first aid to Sgt. Marchione a second fighter came in from nine o'clock and opened fire. The rounds sliced through the section where the wounded photographers were located, wounding Sgt. Marchione for a second time. The navigator Sec. Lt. Thomas D. Robinson rushed back to the rear crew compartment and began administrating first aid to the severely wounded photographers.

As this drama unfolded the intense action in the rear continued. Attacks came from underneath and above *578*. The forward top turrets guns jammed Col. Svore remembered, "The gunner tried so hard to relieve the jamb that his hands bled to such an extent that I thought he had been hit." The rear top turret gunner Sgt. Jamie F. Smart was doing his best to fight off the attackers, when a fighter closed in from three o'clock and filled his sight. Sgt. Smart let loose a burst, and as the rounds slammed into the fighter it rolled over and exploded underneath the Dominator. It was *578*'s third kill in two days.

Success was followed by tragedy, yet again, as from nine o'clock a fighter came in on Sgt. Smart's turret and opened fire as he was turning the turret into the direction of his attacker. Two rounds went through the Plexiglas enclosure of his turret hitting him in the temple and in the forehead knocking him unconscious. The last bastion for the crew of 578 was a thick layer of clouds 1,500 feet below them. Capt. Svore and Lt. Anderson decided to dive, allowing them to outrun their pursuers and hide in the dense cloud cover. The maneuver separated them from *Hobo Queen II,* leaving *578* to fly back to Okinawa alone, on three engines, with three wounded crew members onboard.

During the return flight Sgt. Anthony Marchione unfortunately succumb to his wounds and became the last official United States service member to be killed in action during WWII. The Japanese fighters that were shot down are the last official kills made by American aircraft during the war, a moment in history often overlooked due to the somber milestone also reached on the mission. The Japanese official records claim that no fighters were lost and one Japanese pilot claimed one B-32 was probably destroyed.

Upon their return to Okinawa, the crews began refering to themselves as, "The 312th Kamikaze Group and Julie Kossor made the following remarks in his journal. "Both planes came back, one killed and two wounded, they both have a fifty, fifty chance to live. The B-32 got its rotten "Glory" of shooting down four Jap planes and three probable (kills) in twenty-five minutes of combat. The war was suppo-sed to be over August 15th, but our men are still getting killed. To us it isn't over for some time yet. Nobody's celebratin' *(sic)* "The End" over here, because the war supposed to be over. We do not get combat time for these missions. We get the rotten deal of flyin' 'em *(sic)* on the house. It does not even count for getting medals or getting home sooner."

25 August 1945

The photographic missions continued a week later. Four B-32's; *Hobo Queen II, 528, 534* and *544* left Yontan and were assigned the mission of photographing the Tokyo area. *Hobo Queen II* and *543* aborted the mission due to mechanical issues, leaving *528* and *544* to continue on the mission. Over Tokyo there was no opposition from the ground or the air. However, the weather was the enemy that day and only forty photographs were taken but not of the assigned targets due to cloud cover and the Dominators returned to Okinawa.

The Lady is Fresh undergoing repairs to its number two engine after rejoining the squadron on 20 August 1945. (Authors Collection)

28 August 1945

"Black Tuesday," wrote Julie Kossor in his journal entry for 28 August 1945. This date proved to be tragic for the men of the 386th BS and the B-32 Dominator. The first mission of the day called for two, Dominators; *The Lady is Fresh* and *544* to fly to Atsugi and Tokyo for a special communications mission to broadcast a "special message," as stated in the official history of the 312th BG.

After the cease-fire with Japan commenced all of the B-32's missions were flown with volunteer crews. The previous day, Julie Kossor had been ordered to clean and keep the ball turret on *544* in good shape, "I had it sparkling."

On the morning of 28 August *The Lady is Fresh* was the first to leave. At 0540 *544* began to make its take off run down the runway. It continually gained speed heading down the strip, and just as the pilot, Lt. Leonard M. Sill, was going to lift the nose of *544* into the air the

544 undergoing maintenance at Yontan, another B-32 is directly behind it.
(Authors Collection)

number three engine sputtered. Lt. Sill opted not to attempt the take off on three engines and he and his co-pilot, Lt. Glen W. Bowie, decreased the throttles and applied the breaks. The Dominator screeched down the runway as it tried desperately to stop. However one distinct sound was missing, the roar of the engines as the pitch of the propellers was reversed. Suddenly, the screeching came to an abrupt halt as *544,* loaded with thirteen crewmen and 7,960 gal of fuel, nose dived seventy feet into a coral pit at the end of the runway.

A split second of silence gave way to a cataclysmic explosion, which was felt throughout the airfield, marking the end of the lives of the thirteen crew members on board. The explosion rocked Yontan and a plume of smoke marking the solemn end of the crew was seen for miles. The larges pieces left of the giant bomber was the left wing.

On board *544* were some of the 386th BS's non flying officers including Woody Houser, an intelligence officer, and Bill Barnes, a communications officer, both were being rewarded for their service thr-

The remains of *544* at the bottom of the coral pit after it slid off the end of the Yontan runway. The largest piece that remained was the left wing. (Authors Collection)

oughout the war. Robert Nova remembered, "They were all great guys, the Doc that cured my jungle rot was on board too. It was a sad day."

The co-pilot Lt. Glen W. Bowie was a former B-24 reconnaissance pilot who transferred into the 386th BS to fly B-32's. A former crewmember remembered in a letter to Lt. Bowie's family, "He flew because he thought it was the right thing to do and because he felt is was safer to fly in combat aircraft with others around to help them than in photo airplanes that flew solo."

Julie Kossor's journal entry read, "All the bodies were burnt and at 1600 were having a church service for them. Odds were six to one it could have been our crew only twelve crews fly B-32's ours is number eleven. My nose gunner grounded himself, I was to but I am waiting to decide."

Another member of the 386th BS was originally slated to be one of the volunteer crewmen on *544*. By a stroke of luck, he spent the previous night playing a hotly contested chess match that lasted into the early morning hours of 28 August. He decided to sleep in late that morning, opting not to go along on the mission, dubiously allowing another volunteer crewmember the opportunity. Jack Munsell was on *528* which was directly behind *544* in the order of takeoff, "Both crews knew each other and this accident was clearly a shocking experience to everyone."

The second mission for the day was another photographic mission that called for three B-32's to fly to Tokyo, *Hobo Queen II*, *528* and *578* were selected for the fourteen hour mission that was intended to leave directly after the first flight. However, due to the unexpected loss of *544*, Jack Munsell remembered, "Our pilot waited an hour and we took off at about 0730. Looking down on the still smoldering debris was not a good way to start the day and I expect we all prayed for out lost comrades, tent mates, buddies and friends." Their mission was to photograph the airfields in the Tokyo area. Each B-32 had a crew of thirteen which included the normal crew and two photographers.

Already en route was *The Lady is Fresh*, which was participating in its first mission since finally rejoining the squadron on 20 August. Just north of Okinawa the crew began to experience some engine troubles and was forced to turn back. As the crew approached the strip at Yontan they passed over the wreckage of *544* and landed just after the other three Dominators had taken off.
On this mission Jack Munsell was who, for reasons unknown, was assigned to fly in the ball turret, which he had never even been in before prior to that day. On the way to the target, "Our flight was uneventful, even in the ball turret where all you could see was the bottom of the airplane and the ground bellow," and as they approached the Tokyo area "We saw no other planes until we neared Tokyo. Some Navy Hellcats came up to look us over and we waved at each other. It felt real good to have friendly company in Japanese territory armed and ready to protect us." They arrived over Atsugi and Tokyo, and assisted with the broadcast of the special message. After assisting with the communications mission the crews completed their intended mission, taking photographs above Tokyo and turned for home. On their way back to Okinawa fate finally caught up with the troubled *528*.

This could possibly be the last photo taken of *528,* sitting on a rain soaked hardstand at Yontan, before it was lost on the final B-32 mission of the war. (Authors Collection)

The radio operator onboard *528* was SSgt Wiley D. Pringle who, just a few days after the mission, wrote a detailed letter to his brother about the events of the flight. "Everything went along fine until 1700 when an engine (No. 2) cut out. No one thought anything about that, because we always fly on three engines in these B-32's." SSgt. Pringle, Sgt. Jack Munsell and the rest of the crew continued the flight thinking about their eventual return to Okinawa until their daydreaming abruptly ended at 1845 when the number four engine died. "We began losing altitude, we threw overboard all of the equipment that could be cut out. By this time we were about 300 miles from our base," wrote SSgt. Pringle.

Jack Munsell remembered, "We were in serious trouble since we could not maintain altitude or air speed necessary for straight and level flight. We threw out all remaining ammunition, the insides of our

126

.50 caliber machine guns, rations, ditching supports, our side arms, all camera equipment, my shoes and the bombs site."

The bomber was still slowly losing altitude as it closed the distance with Okinawa, now only 175 miles away. Jack Munsell remembered thinking to himself as they struggled along, "We weren't going to make it. At this stage we rounded up all of our equipment such as, parachutes, life preservers and life rafts." The pilot, Lt. Collins Orton knew he couldn't hold the bomber from nosing over and diving to the sea for much longer and ordered the crew to bail out at 1903. Jack Munsell took the call in the rear crew compartment from Lt. Orton, "The pilot ordered me to make sure all five crew members in the rear of the plane bailed out on time and that I would notify him when I was the only one left, which I did." He was then ordered to jump himself, "My parachute opened okay, praise the Lord." He also recalled

An undated picture of Wiley Pringle (far right) and other USAAF personnel, unfortunately the identities of the other men have been lost. (Frederickson)

a conversation he once had with a GI about their parachutes, "I was told once that if a chute failed to open it could be returned to the manufacture for replacement."

After Jack Munsell and the others in the rear crew compartment finished bailing out, Lt. Orton then ordered SSgt. Pringle (who was still onboard to radio Yontan giving them *528*'s situation and location while Lt. Orton contacted destroyers that were stationed in the area for the purpose of rescuing downed flyers and informed them to stand by, as his crew had been ordered to bail out.

"I was about the ninth man to go out," wrote SSgt. Pringle. "I went out the bomb bay, the next thing I knew, I was on my back looking up at the plane, I pulled the ripcord. My chute opened okay but I got one hellava *(sic)* jolt. I hit the water hard as hell, but it didn't hurt me". "I inflated my Mae West (life vest) and got my harness off. By this time the parachute was all tangled around my legs. This is a helpless situation, which seemed to last about thirty minutes. While trying to untangle myself, my one-man life raft sank. The China Sea was very rough, the waves were over my head and besides all that there were sharks all around us."

Lt. Orton was the last man out of the stricken bomber. He bailed as the crew was still floating down and some had just hit the water. From each vantage point the crew watched as the pilot less B-32 nosed over and descended rapidly to the sea exploding on impact with the water.

Sgt. Munsell remembers, "One second I was floating down and the next second I was under water. It was slightly after sun set when I managed to inflate my one man raft only to discover it was upside down. I had to get back in the water again to turn it over." As evening was setting in he was still floating in his raft, "I could not see any destroyers, but there was a PBY seaplane flying over. This was great but it could not land and pick me up because the sea was to rough. I was happy to see the PBY because this meant they had our location." Now all he could do was hope that the PBY would be able to land in the morning and pick them if the seas improved by then.

Prior to the loss of *528* there was a service and burial for the men of *544*. All the 386th BS's personnel that had remained at Yontan gathered at the cemetery to say good bye, "They were buried at Yontan cemetery near Ernie Pyles grave," remembered Col. Svore. The service had just ended, and the men were finding their way back to their duties when they "learned another B-32 went down," wrote Julie Kossor.

The late evening dusk rapidly turned to darkness. SSgt. Wiley Pringle, Sgt Jack Munsell and the other men of *528,* still floating in the North China Sea, were anxiously awaiting rescue. Responding to the calls of Lt. Orton were the destroyers *U.S.S. Aulick* and *U.S.S. John D. Henley*. The crew aboard the *Aulick* spotted SSgt Pringle bobbing in the water and sent a whale boat out to pick him up, "It was the most glorious sight I had ever seen I started to swim towards it," after he swam about thirty yards the rescuers reached him and pulled him into the whale boat, "I was as happy as Hell," Wiley Pringle wrote his brother. While Wiley Pringle was being rescued Jack Munsell was trying to pass the time making plans to use his parachute the next day to shield him from the harsh sun and to use his one dye marker in the daylight so he could hope to be spotted by passing aircraft. Suddenly, searchlights appeared on the water. "It went right over me a couple of times. Apparently they did not see me because of the rough seas and because I was four to five miles away. I got out the signal mirror (which was a part of the survival kit in his one man raft) which was supposed to be used in daylight by reflecting the suns rays. I therefore thought about using it to reflect the ships search light glare."

He caught the attention of the crewmembers aboard the destroyer *U.S.S. Aulick,* and a launch was sent out to check on the source of the light. "It seemed like it took the small boat forever to get to my raft." One of the sailors in the boat had a rope tied around him and jumped into the chilly waters and swam for Jack Munsell and, upon his arrival to Jack's raft, the sailors in the boat pulled on the rope pulling the men to the safety of the whale boat for the ride back to the destroyer, ending the day's ordeal. "I am and will forever be grateful."

The *Aulick* rescued nine of the downed crewmembers and the *John D. Henley*, was able to pick up three more. Cpl. Morris C. Morgan a gunner, was missing and hadn't been seen since he had bailed out of the stricken *528*, and was presumed missing. On board the *Aulick* was another gunner, SSgt. George C. Murphy. SSgt. Murphy's chute had tangled as he fell to the water, upon impact he had broken his pelvis. Two hours after being rescued he died of internal injuries and was buried at sea.

Fifteen men of the 386th BS Very Heavy died in one day and a total of sixteen during the month. The surviving crew members of *528* returned to Okinawa after spending a week aboard ship only to find out that as of 1 September 1945 all B-32 combat and training operations had been ordered to conclude and the crews were preparing for their eventual return home.

This unidentified Dominator is parked on a Yontan hardstand awaiting its return to the United States. Only nine B-32's reached the Pacific by the end of the war. (Authors Collection)

The Lady is Fresh parked amongst other aircraft at Yontan, in the back round are B-24's and a Curtis C-46 Commando. (Authors Collection)

CHAPTER 8

WARS END

The end of the WWII rapidly brought about the demise of the B-32 Dominator. On 29 August 1945 the B-32 school and flight training effectively ended when operations were ordered to stop by V Bomber Command. However, training in the United States continued until September, when training finally ceased at FWAAF.

On 31 August 1945 Capt. Svore was directed to fly *530,* which had been repaired after the tough missions over Tokyo back to the United States to deliver photographs of the official Surrender on 2 September 1945 aboard the *U.S.S. Missouri* in Tokyo Bay and for a brief publicity tour. Prior to their departure artwork was added to the forward fuselage, the 5th Air Force emblem and the words *Direct From Tokyo* were painted on both sides of the fuselage and the insignia of the 312th BG, "The Roaring 20's" was painted on the nose just aft of the nose turret. Capt. Svore and the crew were ordered back to the U.S. with Col. Salem Wells, the commanding officer of 312th BG. Their mission was to fly Lt. Col. Selmon Wells to Washington D.C. via New York City to deliver the first set of photographs taken of the surrender ceremony.

Capt. Svore standing next to *Direct From Tokyo,* the B-32 he flew back to the United States once the war was over to deliver photographs of the Japanese formal surrender. (Svore)

After delivering the photographs and Col. Wells to Washington D.C. the crew was then to continue on the publicity tour, making their last stop in Fort Worth at Consolidated's production facility. The flight back to the United States proved to be eventful and nerve racking.

As Capt. Svore, Col. Wells, and the crew of *Direct From Tokyo* reached the west coast of the United States they were greeted home by a line of heavy thunderstorms. Flying at 15,000 feet ice began to accumulate on the wings and the crew experienced St. Elmo's fire (a static electrical buildup that sparks like lighting) on the tips of all four propellers. To make matters worse, the engines were starting to lose power because of ice build up on the carburetors. "It was rough weather and was my first encounter with such heavy icing in the B-32. There was incredible tension," recalled Svore. To combat the ice build up he switched on what he presumed was the carburetor heaters, when suddenly the engines began running rough and *Direct From Tokyo* began rapidly losing altitude.

In fact Capt. Svore had unintentionally toggled the engine oil dilution switches for cold weather starting of the engines and by the time he was able to correct the problem and regain full power to the engines they had lost 7,000 feet of altitude.

The rough weather now behind them, the crew reached their destination, "We had flown around the clock to Washington D.C. and landed at Washington National, I over shot the taxi turnoff as it was a short runway." Instinctively, Capt. Svore reversed the pitch of the two inboard propellers and backed the big bomber back onto the runway, much to the surprise of the men in the control tower, who indicated their surprise in the B-32's ability to back up.

After delivery of the photographs, the next stop was the Consolidated plant in Fort Worth. The publicity tour was cancelled except for the stop in Fort Worth. Just Capt. Svore and his flight engineer were onboard. The intended purpose of the flight was to show off the fruits of the employee's labor over the last year and hopefully boost their morale, since the end of the war threatened the cancellation of further contracts and jeopardized their jobs.

Direct From Tokyo awaiting the return flight to the States. The last time it had been flown was over Tokyo on 17 August. (Authors Collection)

A GI relaxing in front *Direct From Tokyo* serial number *42-108530*, in the back round is the tail of *578*. (Authors Collection)

The last time Capt. Svore flew *Direct From Tokyo* was after leaving Fort Worth in route to Kingman, Arizona to deliver the B-32 to its final resting spot. During the last flight they approached the Grand Canyon. Capt. Svore and his flight engineer decided to take a closer look and took a brief "Joy ride" through the Grand Canyon for several miles. "The war was to recent for this to be a serious flying violation as it would be today," said Capt. Svore. The two delivered *Direct From Tokyo,* expecting to return to Okinawa but were stationed stateside.

With the war over and the B-29 a proven success, the B-32 Dominator was stricken from the USAAF post war inventory. Production ended almost as soon as it began, on 8 September 1945 Consolidated was informed by the USAAF that all B-32's on order were cancelled and on 12 September production formally halted. The only Dominators to be completed were those that were already on the assembly lines, near fully assembled. A total of 117 B-32's and TB-

32's were produced at the Consolidated Fort Worth assembly plant. The three XB-32's and one B-32 were completed at the production facility in San Diego.

The end of the 386th BS came in early October 1945. In the following days the remaining B-32's and their crewmen were prepared in anticipation of their departure for the long awaited trip home. This included gathering personal belongings, saying good bye to friends and readying the aircraft. The ball turrets were removed and artwork was added to some of the B-32's. The 5th AF emblem was painted on the tail of *Hobo Queen II*, *The Lady is Fresh* and *578* had the symbol of the 386th BS, a club, painted on their tails. *543* had a map of Indiana, the

42-108531 never took part in a combat mission but was used for transition training. In the background is *The Lady is Fresh* with a club (the insignia of the 386th BS) painted on its tail. These two B-32's had their ball turrets removed and the openings for the machine guns on the nose and tail turrets taped over. (Authors Collection)

Hobo Queen II quietly awaited its fait on a Yontan hardstand, after a nose gear collapse failed repair attempts caused it to be deemed un-flyable. (Authors Collection)

name *Harriet's Chariot* and the names of fifteen crew members painted on the left fuselage. On 10 October the *Hobo Queen II* was on its takeoff run when the nose gear collapsed causing slight damage. Maintenance personnel on Okinawa attempted to repair the nose gear but caused further damage to the aircraft when it was dropped from its hoist not once but twice. Unfortunately, due to the further damage caused during the repair efforts *Hobo Queen II* remained on Okinawa and was eventually scrapped in May 1946. The day of departure for the flight crews of the 386th BS came on 16 October 1945. The veteran B-32's were flown directly to the Reconstruction Finance Corporation (RFC) center established at Kingman, Arizona joining *Direct From Tokyo* and the other B-32's and TB-32's that had already been sent there.

B-32's fresh off the assembly line sat next to combat veteran and crew trainers at the RFC centers located at Kingman and Walnut Ridge, Arkansas awaiting potential buyers. There were a total of

42-108540 was on display with a collection of aircraft including a C-54 to its right, a C-97 directly behind, and a B-29 in front of it, at Wright AAF in October 1945. (Authors Collection)

The last B-32 *42-108474* parked at Freeman AAF, Indiana awaiting the completion of the proposed United States Army Air Force Museum. Eventually the last Dominator was flown to Kingman AAF for storage until the museum was completed but was scrapped in 1949. (USAAF)

eighty-seven slightly used and brand new B-32's flown to Walnut Ridge and thirty-seven were sent to Kingman. The price of a surplus B-32 was $32,500 compared to $790,000 it cost the War Department at the time of production. Unfortunately no one was interested in the B-32 and over a two year period, 1946 and 1947 all the B-32's in storage except for one were scrapped.

The last B-32 serial number *42-108474* was designated for future use in the USAAF museum but eventually met the fate of all the other Dominators. The only portions of the B-32's to survive intact were the Curtis Electric propellers, the eighteen and one half-foot propellers were removed during scrapping and replaced the Hamilton Standards on the USAAF's remaining B-29's.

The legacy of the B-32 Dominator remains with the men whose lives were impacted most by the bomber. Col. Svore, the only B-32 Squadron Commander was, "Sorry that the plane did not have a post war role." Robert Nova, the representative from the Sperry Gyro Scope Company and B-32 School instructor, said that, "The airplane never really got recognized for what it was." Robert Kirk, the B-32 pilot in training at FWAAF, said it was "A superior aircraft which came on the scene to late, and disheartened to see them flown into storage." Finally, Wayne Grooms the B-32 senior instructor and veteran B-24 pilot said, "I felt fortunate to fly this aircraft, I liked it very much. Later I had flown the B-29 and other aircraft that were not as responsive to the controls". This was a feeling shared by many who came in contact with the B-32, including the trainee pilots at Tarrant Field who gave many glowing reviews in their base news paper, the *Tarantaneer*, "A sweet airplane, fast and agile, the crews are impressed with the ease in which the B-32 takes to the air."

Unfortunately when the last Dominator was scrapped the bombers brief but important history went with it. Today all that remains are collections of old photographs, oddball parts and the echoes of the men who flew the Consolidated B-32 Dominator.

(Above and Below) 87 B-32's used for training, testing and those fresh off the assembly line were sent to RFC Walnut Ridge. (USAAF)

(Above and Below) These, Dominators were used at Fort Worth as fully equipped crew trainers. The 4M number codes on the fuselage were field identification numbers assigned to each B-32 at FWAAF. (USAAF)

ORIGINAL USAAF PRODUCTION SCHEDULE

Quantity	Date
1	September, 1943
2	October, 1943
5	November, 1943
8	December, 1943
11	January, 1944
14	February, 1944
18	March, 1944
22	April, 1944
26	May, 1944
30	June, 1944
35	July, 1944
40	August, 1944
45	September, 1944
43	October, 1944

REVISED PRODUCTION SCHEDULE

Quantity	Date
1	April, 1944
2	May, 1944
5	June, 1944
8	July, 1944
11	August, 1944
14	September, 1944
18	October, 1944
22	November, 1944
26	December, 1944
30	January, 1945
35	February, 1945
40	March, 1945
45	April, 1945
45	May, 1945
11	June, 1945

B-32 PRODUCTION BY MONTH

1944

August	2
September	1
October	0
November	1
December	12

1945

January	7
February	17
March	18
April	11
May	17
June	21
July	8
August	3

B-32 HISTORY BY SERIAL NUMBER

XB-32 San Diego

41-141, Lindberg Field, Crashed (Engine Failure), 5/10/43

41-142, Lindberg Field/Muroc AAF, Scrapped

41-18336, Lindberg Field/ Wright AAF, Scrapped

B-32-1-CF

42-108471, Used by Consolidated as test aircraft, Scrapped

42-108472, Crashed (Hydraulic Failure), 9/19/44

42-108473, Wright AAF, Used for flight tests, Destroyed in fire

42-108474, "4", ATSC, RFC Kingman

42-108475, FWAAF, Crashed (Engine Fire), 4/10/45

42-108476, "6", ASTC, Squadron E, 611th BS, AAFPGC, RFC Walnut Ridge

42-108477, 4M74, 2519th AAFBU, 581, Squadron E, 611th BS, AAFPGC, RFC Walnut Ridge

42-108478, ATSC, RFC Walnut Ridge

42-108479, Wright AAF, Static Test Model, Scrapped

42-108480, AFFTC, RFC Kingman

B-32-5-CF

42-108481, ATSC, RFC Walnut Ridge

42-108482, ATSC, RFC Walnut Ridge

42-108483, "03", ATSC, 4M97, 2519th AAFBU, Scrapped

42-108484- 4M75 2519th AAFBU, 580, Squadron E, 611th BS, AAFPGC, RFC Walnut Ridge

TB-32-5-CF

42-108485, OM17, 2519th AAFBU, RFC Kingman

42-108486, Written Off

42-109487, OM10, 2519th AAFBU, Scrapped

42-108488, OM12, 2519th AAFBU, RFC Kingman

42-108489, "1", K-199, K-510, Destroyed in Crash

42-108490, OM13, 2519th AAFBU, Scrapped

42-108491, OM14, 2519th AAFBU, Scrapped

42-108492, OM15, 2519th AAFBU, Scrapped

42-108493, OM35, 2519th AAFBU, RFC Kingman
42-108494, OM29, 2519th AAFBU, Scrapped
42-108495, OM34, 2519th AAFBU, Crashed (Engine Fire) 3/8/45
TB-32-10-CF
42-108496, OM18, 2519th AAFBU, Scrapped
42-108497, OM16, 2519th AAFBU, RFC Kingman
42-108498, OM37, 2519th AAFBU, Scrapped
42-108499, OM28, 2519th AAFBU, Crashed 5/4/45
42-108500, OM20, 2519th AAFBU, RFC Kingman
42-108501, OM19, 2519th AAFBU, Scrapped
42-108502, OM34, 2519th AAFBU, Scrapped
42-108503, OM21, 2519th AAFBU, Scrapped
42-108504, OM38, 2519th AAFBU, Scrapped
42-108505, OM22, 2519th AAFBU, Scrapped
42-108506, OM27, 2519th AAFBU, Scrapped
42-108507, OM25, 2519th AAFBU, RFC Kingman
42-108508, OM39, 2519th AAFBU, Scrapped
42-108509, OM32, 2519th AAFBU, Scrapped
42-108510, OM24, 2519th AAFBU, Scrapped
42-108511, OM11, 2519th AAFBU, Scrapped
42-108512, OM23, 2519th AAFBU, Scrapped
42-108513, OM13, 2519th AAFBU, Scrapped
42-108514, OM40, 2519th AAFBU, Scrapped
42-108515, OM36, 2519th AAFBU, Scrapped
42-108516, OM44, 2519th AAFBU, Scrapped
42-108517, OM31, 2519th AAFBU, Scrapped
42-108518, OM30, 2519th AAFBU, Scrapped
42-108519, OM33, 2519th AAFBU, Scrapped
42-108520, OM41, 2519th AAFBU, Scrapped
TB-32-15-CF
42-108521, OM28, 2519th AAFBU, Scrapped
42-108522, OM45 (OM12), 2519th AAFBU, Scrapped
42-108523, OM42, 2519th AAFBU, Scrapped
42-108524, OM43 (OM10), 2519th AAFBU, Scrapped

B-32-20-CF
42-108525, ATSC, RFC Walnut Ridge
42-108526, ATSC, RFC Walnut Ridge
42-108528, 312th BG, 386th BS, Crashed (Engine Failure) 8/28/45
42-108529, *The Lady is Fresh* 312th BG, 386th BS, RFC Kingman
42-108530, *Direct From Tokyo*, 312th BG, 386th BS, RFC Kingman
42-108531, 312th BG, 386th BS, RFC Kingman
42-108532, *Hobo Queen II*, 312th BG, 386th BS, Written Off (Nose Gear Failure) 10/10/45
42-108533, AFFTC, RFC Walnut Ridge
42-108534, AFFTC, RFC Walnut Ridge
42-108535, ATSC/AFFTC, 589, Squadron E, 611th BS, AAFPGC, RFC Walnut Ridge
42-108536, AFFTC, RFC Walnut Ridge
42-108537, AFFTC, RFC Kingman
42-108538, AFFTC, RFC Walnut Ridge
42-108539, 312th BG, 386th BS, Written Off (Battle Damage) 8/17/45
42-108540, ATSC, Wight AAF, RFC Walnut Ridge
42-108541, ATSC, RFC Walnut Ridge
42-108542, ATSC, RFC Walnut Ridge
42-108543, "Harriet's Chariot," 312th BG, 386th BS, RFC Kingman
42-108544, 312th BG, 386th BS, Crashed (Engine Failure), 8/28/45
42-108545, Scrapped
B-32-21-CF
42-108527, Used as Paratrooper Conversion Test Bed, FWAAF, Scrapped
B-32-25-CF
42-108546, ATSC, RFC Walnut Ridge
42-108547, 591, Squadron E, 611th BS, AAFPGC, RFC Walnut Ridge
42-108548, 426th AAFBU, 4M87, 2519th AAFBU, RFC Walnut Ridge
42-108549, 426th AAFBU, 4M86, 2519th AAFBU, RFC Walnut Ridge
42-108550, 426th AAFBU, 4M90, 2519th AAFBU, RFC Walnut Ridge

42-108551, 4M91, 2519th AAFBU, RFC Walnut Ridge
42-108552, 426th AAFBU, 4M85, 2519th AAFBU, RFC Walnut Ridge
42-108553, 4M99, 2519th AAFBU, RFC Walnut Ridge
42-108554, 426th AAFBU, 4M84, 2519th AAFBU, RFC Walnut Ridge
42-108555, 4M96, 2519th AAFBU, RFC Walnut Ridge
42-108556, 4M94, 2519th AAFBU, RFC Walnut Ridge
42-108557, 4M95, 2519th AAFBU, RFC Walnut Ridge
42-108558, 4M92, 2519th AAFBU, RFC Walnut Ridge
42-108559, 4M18, 2519th AAFBU, RFC Walnut Ridge
42-108560, 4M83, 2519th AAFBU, RFC Walnut Ridge
42-108561, 4M89, 2519th AAFBU, RFC Walnut Ridge
42-108562, 4M88, 2519th AAFBU, RFC Walnut Ridge
42-108563, 4M76, 2519th AAFBU, RFC Walnut Ridge
42-108564, 4M82, 2519th AAFBU, RFC Walnut Ridge
42-108565, 4M98, 2519th AAFBU, RFC Walnut Ridge
42-108566, 4M81, 2519th AAFBU, RFC Walnut Ridge
42-108567, 4M80, 2519th AAFBU, RFC Walnut Ridge
42-108568, 4M79, 2519th AAFBU, RFC Walnut Ridge
42-108569, 4M78, 2519th AAFBU, RFC Walnut Ridge
42-108570, 4M77, 2519th AAFBU, RFC Walnut Ridge

B-32-30-CF
42-108571, ATSC, RFC Walnut Ridge
42-108572, ATSC, RFC Walnut Ridge
42-108573, ATSC, RFC Walnut Ridge
42-108574, ATSC, 596, Squadron E, 611th BS, AAFPGC, RFC Kingman
42-108575, ATSC, RFC Walnut Ridge
42-108576, ATSC, RFC Walnut Ridge
42-108577, RFC Kingman

B-32-35-CF
42-108578, 312th BG, 386th BS, RFC Kingman
42-108579, RFC Kingman
42-108580, AFFTC, RFC Walnut Ridge
42-108581, Scrapped

42-108582, Scrapped
42-108583, Scrapped
42-108584, Scrapped
B-32-CF
42-108585, Completed to Flyable Status, RFC Walnut Ridge
42-108586, Completed to Flyable Status, RFC Walnut Ridge
42-108587, Completed to Flyable Status, RFC Walnut Ridge
42-108588, Completed to Flyable Status, RFC Walnut Ridge
42-108589, Completed to Flyable Status, RFC Walnut Ridge
42-108590, Completed to Flyable Status, RFC Walnut Ridge
42-108591, Completed to Flyable Status, RFC Walnut Ridge
42-108592, Completed to Flyable Status, RFC Walnut Ridge
42-108593, Completed to Flyable Status, RFC Walnut Ridge
42-108594, Completed to Flyable Status, RFC Walnut Ridge
B-32's Destroyed Before Completion at Fort Worth
42-108595 - 42-108644
Cancelled (Fort Worth)
42-108645 – 42-108770
B-32-20-CO (San Diego)
44-90486, RFC, Kingman
44-90487, Completed to Flyable Status, RFC Kingman
44-90488, Completed to Flyable Status, RFC Kingman
Cancelled (San Diego)
44-90489 – 90985

KEY
ATSC - Air Technical Service Center
AAFPGC - Army Air Force Proving Ground Center
AAFTC - Army Air Force Tactical Center
426th AAFBU – Mountain Home Army Air Field
2519th AAFBU – Fort Worth Army Air Field
OM, Identification numbers of TB-32's assigned to Fort Worth Army
    Air Field
4M, Identification numbers of B-32's assigned to Fort Worth Army
    Air Field

Bibliography

Books
Chinnery, Philip, D, *50 Years of the Desert Boneyard*, MBI, Osceola, WI, 1995.
Harding, Steven & Long, James, *Dominator: The Story of the Consolidated B-32 Bomber,* Pictorial Histories, MT, 1984.
Veronico, Nicholas, A, Grantham, A, Kevin & Thompson, Scott, *Military Aircraft Boneyards*, MBI, Osceola, WI, 2000.

Magazines and Newspapers
Consolidated Vultee News, "AAF Reveals B-32 in Action Against Japs," 3 August 1945.
Harding, Steven, "Dominator," *Air Classics*, December, 1991.
Hutchenson, James, E, B-32 Bomber Hits From Luzon Bases," *New York Times,* "29 July 1945.
Johnsen, Fredrick, A, "Last and Unluckiest of the Hemisphere Bombers," *Wings,* February, 1974.
Kluckhohn, Frank, L, "Japanese Attack B-32's over Tokyo," *New York Times,* 18 August 1945.
Kluckhohn, Frank, L, "Big B-32 Crippled," *New York Times,* 19 August 1945.

Munsell, Jack S, "Dominator Mission," *The Friends Journal,* Summer 2000.

New York Times, AP, "Super-Bomber Named Dominator," 25 August 1944.

New York Times, UP, "Most of Yokohama Smashed." 31 May 1945.

Philadelphia Record, "B-32's Attacked on Mission Near Yokohama," 18 August 1945.

Sack, Thomas, L, Maj. (USAF), "About that B-32 on Our Front Cover," *Air Force Magazine,* September, 1980.

Tarranteer, Vol. 3, No. 24, August 1, 1945. Official Newspaper of FWAAF.

Whittaker, Wayne, "Here's the B-32-Our Newest Super Bomber, *Popular Mechanics*, September, 1945.

White, William, S, "17,000 Planes Cut Off Army Program, Saving 4 Billion," *New York Times,* 26 May 1945.

Y'Blood, William, "Second String," *AAHS Journal*, Summer, 1968.

Microfilm
USAF Archives: Microfilm B0231, "312th Bomb Group History," AFSHRC, Maxwell AFB, AL.

USAF Archives: Microfilm A0597, "386th, 387th and 388th Bomb Squadron History," AFSHRC, Maxwell AFB, AL.

USAF Archives: Microfilm A7508, 5th Air Force Bomber Command History, April-June 1945, AFSHRC, Maxwell AFB,   AL.

USAF Archives: Microfilm, A7509, 5th Air Force Bomber Command History July-August 1945, AFSHRC, Maxwell AFB, AL.

USAF Archives: Microfilm, ACR-77, B-32 Record Cards Serial Numbers 42-108471 – 584, AFSHRC, Maxwell AFB, AL.

Personal Narratives
Arendsee, Roger, Correspondence with Author 2003.

Eidnes, Ken, Correspondence with Author, 2003.

Grooms, Wayne, Correspondences with Author, 2003.

Kirk, Robert, E, Correspondence with Author, 2005.

Kossor, Julius, Personal Journal, 1945, Courtesy of the Online Justin Museum of Military History, 2007.

Nova, Robert, Correspondences with Author, 2003.

Pringle, Wiley, Correspondence with Brother, 1945, Courtesy of Nita Fredrickson, 2007.

Svore, Col. F.L., Correspondences with Author, 2003-2004.

www.ingramcontent.com/pod-product-compliance
Lightning Source LLC
Chambersburg PA
CBHW021336090426
42742CB00008B/631